MAKING
Contracts

MAKING
Contracts

Agreements to buy or supply

BARRIE HAWKINS
WITH GRANT BAGE

**KOGAN
PAGE**

First published in 1991

Apart from any fair dealing for the purposes of research or private study, or
criticism or review, as permitted under the Copyright, Designs and Patents Act,
1988, this publication may only be reproduced, stored or transmitted, in any
form or by any means, with the prior permission in writing of the publishers, or
in the case of reprographic reproduction in accordance with the terms of licences
issued by the Copyright Licensing Agency. Enquiries concerning reproduction
outside those terms should be sent to the publishers at the undermentioned
address:

Kogan Page Limited
120 Pentonville Road
London N1 9JN

© Barrie Hawkins and Grant Bage 1991

British Library Cataloguing in Publication Data
A CIP record for this book is available from the British Library.
ISBN 0-7494-0212-1

Printed and bound in Great Britain by
Clays Limited, St Ives plc

Contents

Preface

'If only I'd known that...'

The corner grocery shop and ICI are more dissimilar than they are alike, but they both face *this* problem: like a magnet, their business operations draw in a multitude of documentation *full of legal implications*.

Some of this may appear quite innocuous: a piece of paper for example headed 'Acknowledgement of Order'. It may seem so inconsequential that you neither bother to read it nor consider it, even if you are asked to sign it. On the other hand, some documentation makes you uncomfortably aware of its gravity by the numerous paragraphs of small print referring to matters you do not understand; or perhaps it is entitled 'Contract'. But it is so off-putting to read and much of it won't make sense and you've a lot to do today . . .

Arrangements to buy or supply are contracts. The paperwork involved therefore has contractual implications: it is creating legal obligations and rights. The document may not be entitled 'Contract' or 'Acknowledgement of Order.' It may be entitled 'Quotation', 'Terms of Trading', 'Notice', 'Agreement', 'Delivery Note', 'Order Form', 'Estimate', or almost anything else the other party chooses to call it. Perhaps it is a letter. It may be so familiar to you from constant sighting that you never give it a thought. If you do glance at it perhaps you are comforted by the thought that you have never had any problems with it.

However, pick up any example of an unconsidered paper headed 'Agreement' or 'Terms of Trading' or 'Conditions of Supply' or something similar. In your hand you will be holding a document full of legal implications.

Aims of this book

Whether you are an employee or run your own business, in the private or the public sector, *Making Contracts* will help you to:

- appreciate at what stage the organisation becomes legally bound in its transactions;
- imbue dealings with clarity so that all sides know what to expect;
- understand the documentation received by your organisation from suppliers and customers;
- see the need for your organisation to have its own documentation and the sort of matters that should be covered;
- ensure that the organisation is acting within the law and in its own best interests;
- avoid mistakes that could lead to costly litigation.

Contracts come in all shapes, sizes and types. Our criterion for deciding what types of contract the book should cover has been: 'What contracts might any business expect to make on a daily basis?' So our concern is with contracts for the sale and purchase of goods, for the supply of services, and for work and materials, considering both the organisation's suppliers and its customers. Some fields of activity, such as building construction, civil engineering and shipping, have their own specialised contracts which take them outside our scope.

This practical guide gives numerous examples of contractual clauses typical of those that could be encountered daily by any business. Our vehicle for this is a fictional case study which commences on page 73 and scrutinises a number of contracts made over the course of a working week by one particular business.

We have also included a number of real-life case histories, drawn from court reports. Let what happened to others be a guide to you.

Making Contracts will help you to understand the documentation showered on your business by suppliers and customers, at the same time giving you insight into the complexities involved in devising your own terms, and the realisation that such a task almost certainly calls for expert assistance.

What you will learn from *Making Contracts* will cut down the time spent with lawyers in devising the contents of your documentation. You will be alert to the sort of matters that should be covered; you will be more able to provide them with the information they need and to communicate with them.

Making Contracts will help *you* to help *them* devise the most effective documentation for your business.

There are many important legal considerations inherent in the process of making agreements to buy or supply goods or services. You will learn how to make and understand legally binding agreements, and in so doing help to avoid legal problems.

Some words of caution

The practice of law and the practice of medicine have much in common: they are both services provided by highly skilled and trained professionals. A book on healthy living written for the lay person might help you, the reader, to avoid a heart attack but it will not turn you into a doctor; nor can one book turn you into a lawyer. As a guide for the non-lawyer, the book has to be written in general terms and is intended as an introduction to the main legal issues involved. In particular, please bear in mind that the situations in the case histories and examples may not be identical to your own. All reasonable care has been taken in preparing the text but neither the authors nor the publisher can accept responsibility for any loss, however caused, that arises from reliance placed on the material in the book, nor for any errors that remain. As the law can change, we have endeavoured to state the law as it stood in April 1991.

That said, we hope that just as a book on healthy living might help prevent a heart attack, so too *Making Contracts* will help you avoid its legal equivalent.

Where the law is concerned, ignorance is *not* bliss.

Chapter 1

What Is a Contract?

There can be few subjects about which there are more popular misconceptions than the law of contract, yet its rules govern much of our everyday lives. It lays down your legal position whenever you buy or sell something. It is not just concerned with the selling of goods, however, but also sets out your legal rights and duties when you have work performed for you, or you undertake work for others.

During the course of our personal and professional lives all of us agree things with other people; we make many agreements. We agree to meet a friend for lunch, we agree to take the children out while our other half does the hoovering, we agree with the plumber he will install our new bathroom, we agree 9 am delivery of urgent packages with a courier service. We make dozens of agreements during an average week.

Clearly, some of these we would not want to hold the other party to in a court of law: it probably does not matter that much if our friend is late or the hoovering is forgotten. But in some cases it may matter a great deal if the other party does not stick to what was agreed: we hope the agreements will be binding. In such a case, what we are in fact hoping is that the agreement is a contract, for that is what a contract is: *a legally binding agreement*.

Check your legal knowledge

Here are ten statements concerned with some fundamental principles of contract law. Which of them if any, are true, and which if any, are false? Tick the relevant box for each and check your answers when you have finished all ten.

This self-test is to help determine how prone you are to a sudden legal pain. If you get any wrong answers, it will help to concentrate your mind on what you need to know. Answer honestly but quickly, and complete it on your own.

	True	False

1. *To be enforceable in a court of law a contract must generally be in writing.* ☐ ☐

2. *A contract for the sale of goods will be upheld by the courts only if a deposit has been paid.* ☐ ☐

3. *If goods on display in a store window are wrongly underpriced, the customer can insist that the shop sell the goods at the price displayed.* ☐ ☐

4. *The court would consider it unjust and refuse to enforce an agreement to sell something at a fraction of its real value.* ☐ ☐

5. *A wife cannot make a contract with her husband.* ☐ ☐

6. Alan, an accountant, offers his old computer to a client, Tony, for £500. Tony says he'll give Alan £400 for it, which Alan refuses. Tony is now prepared to pay the original asking price, but Alan now wants to keep it as a standby.
As he has offered it already at £500, Alan must sell it at that price. ☐ ☐

7. Nicola sends a letter to a holiday cottage letting agency, making a booking of a cottage for which she has received details, and setting out all the necessary information, including price. The agency replies by post confirming the letting, but their letter is lost in the post.
No contract can have come into being. ☐ ☐

8. Alice offers to sell an antique table to Mary for £750. Mary decides she is not interested and mentions it to her friend Giles, an antique dealer. He pops round and leaves a note at Alice's house saying he will have the table and enclosing the cash.
This is binding on Alice. ☐ ☐

9. An entertainment agency offers a chain of stores the services of a well-known soap star to open a new branch. It says it will keep the offer open for seven days. After three days the agency tells the company it has committed the star to another function and is therefore withdrawing its offer.

	True	False

The offer cannot be withdrawn until the time stipulated has lapsed. ☐ ☐

10. Mike asks Fiona what she will give him for his Ford Escort. Fiona replies: 'I'm very fond of you – isn't that enough?' Mike agrees it is and promises to hand over the car. He has now changed his mind.
This is a binding agreement. ☐ ☐

In fact, all ten statements are false.

No, you do not have to have paid a deposit for it to be a contract. No, as a general rule, an agreement does not have to be in writing.

Common sense will often help you to decide which agreements are legally binding and which are not. Let us suppose you purchase an expensive item of stereo equipment and on getting it home cannot get a sound out of it. You take it back to the store and the assistant claims there is nothing you can do about it. You will think to yourself, this can't be right. I must have legal rights here. And of course you do have rights – contractual rights. On the other hand, if you promise to bring your spouse breakfast in bed and then fail to deliver, you would be right in thinking you would not be able to be sued in a court of law.

But in most cases you need to know *exactly* what makes an agreement legally binding.

To get a court to accept that your agreement is not just an agreement, but a contract, you must satisfy the court that three essential ingredients were present: agreement, intention to be bound and consideration. If one is missing you may well have an agreement, but it is not a contract.

1. *Agreement*
   If you are going to law and claiming a legally binding agreement, the first and most obvious thing you must prove is agreement – that the parties *agreed*.
2. *Intention to be bound*
   You are trying to show that there existed a legally binding agreement, so you must convince the court that not only did you make an agreement, but that it was *intended* to be a legally binding one. In other words, the parties intended this should be an agreement to which they could be held in a court of law.

3. *Consideration*

'Consideration' is an example of an everyday word which has a generally understood meaning but to which lawyers attach their own particular meaning. From now onwards, for you, the word consideration does not mean being kind or thoughtful. Henceforth it is a legal term denoting the third essential ingredient required to make an agreement legally binding. It is explained in greater detail on pages 22–4.

Wherever possible, we shall avoid lawyers' jargon; plain English and legal knowledge are not necessarily incompatible!

Chapter 2

The Essentials of a Contract

Agreement

In order to persuade a court that someone else – the other party – agreed with you, you must try to show that their mind was identical with yours.

Let us take the sale of a car as an example. The owner shows the car to the other party and says, 'Here's my Mercedes. If you want it, the price is £5000, delivery on Friday, cash on delivery.' If the other party says, 'Yes', an agreement exists. The parties' minds are identical on the matter: they are both talking about the Mercedes, they both know what the price is, they both know when delivery will be, they both know when payment is to be made. The first thing then to show, when holding someone to a contract, is that the parties' minds were in agreement.

Yet how can you prove such a thing? How can anybody show that what was in one person's mind was the same as was in another's? The answer is that you cannot. So what do lawyers do?

This is a superb example of the limits of the law: we cannot achieve what we ideally want. The answer is to settle for less – and lawyers do this by devising tests which, if satisfied, justify the court holding that there was an agreement.

There is no alternative to this compromise. We cannot see into the mind, so a mechanical test has to be constructed which we can use to satsify the court's needs as far as possible.

Let us re-define our first essential ingredient. More correctly, it is not 'agreement', but 'it looks as if agreement was made'.

'Looks' to whom? To a reasonable person. The test of agreement is: does it look to a reasonable person as if the parties made an agreement?

This test usually involves two stages. First, the court will look to see if an *offer* was made by one of the parties (the offeror). Second, it will enquire if the other party (the offeree) *accepted* that offer. If the court is satisfied on both counts, then it confirms that an agreement exists. It looks as if there was an agreement – therefore there was!

This process means that the parties could go to court and 'pass' this test when no agreement did in reality exist. One of them may know that their minds were not the same, that they were not in agreement. Instantly we have a breeding ground for cries of injustice. But, as we have already observed, the court and the judge cannot see what was actually in the parties' minds; they can merely look back at the available evidence of what the parties did, what they said or wrote, and the surrounding circumstances – if the test is satisfied that it looks as if agreement was reached, then . . .

There is no alternative to this solution of looking at appearances. How important it is, therefore, to keep in mind when you are dealing with others, that you could be held to what you are saying or writing if it would *look to an outsider* that you are making an agreement.

Offers

We have said the court will be looking for an offer made by one of the parties, so what is an offer?

An offer is a *statement of terms*.

During everyday life we say and write many things. Take for example the following conversation which might be heard in workplaces up and down the land:

> *Trevor:* 'My car's in the garage for a service today. Do you know if anyone lives over my way?'
> *Stuart:* 'I do. But I'm leaving early today – sorry, mate.'

In this conversation no offer, or statement of terms, was made. Isolating other common types of statement can help us to define that an offer is *not*:

- *a statement of fact:* 'My car's in the garage for a service today.'
- *a statement of intention:* 'I'm leaving early today.'
- *a request for information:* 'Do you know if anyone lives over my way?'

Offers are not mere requests for information, nor statements of fact, nor statements as to a person's intention. An offer must be distinguished as more than all these. An offer is *a statement of terms which it appears you are willing to stand by*.

How can you tell whether what you or the other person is saying or writing amounts to a statement of terms? Again, common sense takes us some of the way. When you negotiate to buy a car, for instance, you set out the things you need to agree on: eg how much it will be, when delivery will take place, when and how payment will be made.

You must recognise when something is said or written which could be viewed as an offer. If it amounts to an offer in the eyes of the law, then an acceptance communicated by the other party, a 'yes', *brings the contract into being*. And the parties are legally bound *from the point that the contract came into being*.

The clearest guidance as to what might amount to an offer can be found in actual cases. We will look first at a famous case in which the court had to decide whether or not there had been an offer and an acceptance, and thus an agreement. Typically, the court had to try and extricate an offer from a number of communications passing between the parties. The case is one of the most famous in contract law.

Harvey v Facey (1893)

One side in this dispute was the owner of some property, who received a telegram reading: 'Will you sell us Bumper Hall pen?
Telegraph lowest cash price.' (The property was situated in the West Indies, where the term 'pen' refers to a plantation.)

The owner of the property sent back a telegram, reading: 'Lowest price for Bumper Hall pen £900.'

The owner then received another telegram from the enquirer: 'We agree to buy Bumper Hall pen for £900 asked by you.'

When the owner of the property read this he was taken aback. His reaction in effect was: 'I'm not selling it – I don't want to sell it – I didn't want to sell it!' But the enquirer maintained that there was an agreement – a legally binding agreement.

The dispute worked its way up through the courts to the highest appeal court to which it could go, so obviously both parties were determined, and each was convinced he was right.

The result? Since you now know some basics, decide for yourself. Apply the law to the facts, just as the judge has to do. The owner said in effect: 'I have not made an offer to sell. I have not made a statement of terms.' The enquirer retorted: 'Yes, you did. The telegram that you sent stating the lowest cash price was an offer, which I accepted when I replied.'

In its judgement the court took the view that the telegram sent by the owner – the one that read, 'Lowest price for Bumper Hall pen £900' – did not amount to a statement of terms. The court interpreted the telegram as merely stating the price the owner woud accept *if* he was prepared to sell. He was not saying the property *was* for sale. The plaintiff had contended that by stating the price the owner was impliedly answering the question, 'Will you sell us?' in the affirmative. But the court felt that here, especially, the offer must be explicit because land was involved, the complexities in the purchase of which are considerable. It wanted clear evidence of the fact that the alleged vendor intended to bind himself in the negotiations.

If, like the parties here, you pursued your case to the highest appeal court, the legal costs today would be likely to exceed £30,000 and probably be much more. How important it is to know exactly when an offer is being made, either by you or by the other party.

We can clarify an offer by examining what the courts have said does *not* constitute an offer.

Displaying goods for sale

Displaying goods that are for sale does not amount to making an offer to sell.

If you park your car on the driveway of your house with a 'For Sale' notice on the windscreen, it is not a statement of terms by which you are willing to be bound. It is an example of *displaying* goods that are for sale, something you do to encourage people to come forward and negotiate. It is an example of an *invitation to treat*, not an offer. It is an invitation to others to negotiate, or to make offers. It will set the ball rolling.

Police v Bell (1960)

During the 1950s the newspapers were full of stories about 'Teddy Boys', the equivalent perhaps of what today's media call lager louts. In response to public alarm the government passed The Restriction of Offensive Weapons Act. This made it an offence to 'offer for sale' the playthings of the Teddy Boys, their flick-knives. One Mr Bell, who had a shop, made a display of flick-knives in the window, and put a price ticket with them: 'Flick-knives 5 shillings'. The police saw this and Mr Bell was duly charged with contravening the Act by offering flick-knives for sale.

The case was heard by the local magistrates, after which there was an appeal to the High Court. The judgement: Mr Bell was not guilty of offering flick-knives for sale. The court said that the display in the shop window was not an offer to sell the flick-knives, it was a mere invitation to treat, something to attract the attention of passers-by, to help entice them into the shop.

In the case of a sale in a shop, the legal breakdown is that if the customer walks into the shop and says, 'I'll have one of those please,' it is the customer who makes the offer.

Since in this example it is the customer who is making the offer, the shop is free to accept or reject it. The assistant will normally be only too pleased to take the money, but on occasions he or she may not wish to do so. The assistant may have good reasons for not selling an item to a particular customer: for example, it is reserved for somebody else, or it is the only one in stock and is needed for display purposes. The principle is based therefore on sound commercial sense – like so much of our law once you know it.

Advertisements

The courts have usually taken the view that advertisements in newspapers and magazines are also invitations to treat, not offers.

Most of us shop at various times by mail order. Let us suppose your eye is caught by one of the advertisements in the small squares that appear in the papers, particularly at weekends – an advertisement for Afghan slipper socks, say, in *The Guardian.* Such an advertisement does not amount in law to an offer. It is you, the customer, that makes the offer when you write your letter saying, 'Please send me . . .', and enclosing a cheque. The mail order company is free to accept or reject this offer.

Again, it is good common sense. The company may have imported 10,000 pairs of slipper socks from Afghanistan. It cannot know how many orders it will receive. If the law *was* that the advertisement amounted to an offer which was accepted by the customer placing an order, it would mean that if the company, for example, received 11,000 orders it would be in breach of contract 1000 times! It is commercial common sense that the company should be able to reject orders, and it can do this because it is the customer that is making the offer. If the company does receive more orders than it is able to supply, it will inform the customer of the position and return the cheque. In the eyes of the law it is rejecting an offer made by a customer.

Police v Crittenden (1968)

The Protection of Wild Birds Act made it an offence to offer wild birds for sale. Mr Crittenden inserted an advertisement in a fortnightly journal, *Cage and Aviary Birds*. The ad, placed in the classified columns, read 'Bramblefinch cocks and hens 25 shillings each'. Mr Crittenden was prosecuted for offering for sale a wild bird contrary to the Act. *The court held* that the defendant was not guilty. The advertisement constituted merely an invitation to treat and not an offer to sell.

All this is not to say that an advertisement is *incapable* of being an offer. Of course it is possible for an advertiser, if he so chooses, to frame his advertisement in such a way that it does amount to an offer, but there are very few cases where the court has found this to be so. It seems the courts only hold an advertisement to have made a definite offer if it requires readers to go and *do something* for the advertiser, such as '£10 reward if you find and return my lost dog'. It would make such advertisements unworkable if the advertiser could turn round and say 'No, thank you' after the dog was returned, and give it back to the finder!

Circulars and price lists

The courts are likely to take the view that catalogues, circulars and price lists are invitations to treat and not offers.

It is the customer who makes the offer, for example, when completing an order form and posting it, or telephoning a supplier and leaving an order on their telephone answering machine. Again, it enables the supplier to accept or reject the offer if the goods are out of stock, or the customer did not pay the last invoice.

Acceptance

Having decided that one party made an offer, the court then looks to see if the other party accepted that offer. Making the decision to accept is not enough. The fact that you are accepting must be made known to the other party. The contract comes into being, and the parties are bound, at the point at which an acceptance is made known to the party who made the offer.

You can only validly accept an offer if it is made to *you*. The person who makes the offer, the offeror, can make the offer to the whole world if he so wishes, or restrict it to a number of offerees, or make the offer to just one party. If the offer is not made to you, your purported acceptance is in fact an offer, which, like any other offer, the person to whom it is made is free to accept or reject. Thus in this situation no contract has yet come into being (and may not do so), whereas if the offer had been made to you, your acceptance, once communicated, would have brought a contract into being.

To make a valid acceptance, the offer must still be in existence when you endeavour to accept it. An offer comes to an end by being withdrawn by the offeror, for whatever reason, but since the revocation has no validity unless you have been informed of it, you should not find yourself accepting an offer only to be told that it was withdrawn. What is possible is that you attempt to accept an offer that has withered away and died of old age: if it is not accepted an offer will lapse after a period of time. So for how long does a particular offer endure? There is no set period: each case depends on its facts. If an acquaintance offers to sell you his car and you ask for a while to think it over, it would not be a valid acceptance if in six months' time you tell him you've decided to have it! A judge would say that an offer lapses after a reasonable time, and whatever a reasonable time was in this example, six months has certainly exceeded it.

To avoid uncertainty as to whether an offer is still alive, and can therefore be validly accepted, the offeror may choose to put an express time limit on the offer, eg 30 days, after which there can be no acceptance.

Is the agreement legally binding?

Having shown the court that an agreement has been made, you now need to demonstrate that it was intended to be legally binding. Immediately we return to a familiar problem: how can you prove what was actually in the parties' minds, their intention, when the agreement was made? Here again the courts use their trusted friend, the reasonable person – until recently the reasonable *man*. The court again employs the test: what would a reasonable person think? If a reasonable person had heard what was said, knew the background against which the transaction took place, saw what was happening, what would he or she think? Would this bystander come to the conclusion that the parties intended the agreement to be binding?

It is possible for an agreement between members of a family to be a contract if the reasonable person test can be satisfied. You can, if both parties so wish, make a contract even with your spouse. With business transactions, the court *presumes* there is an intention to create legal relations. That is to say, where you have a commercial transaction the court will assume that it was intended to have legal consequences unless one of the parties can convince it otherwise. In practice it is very difficult to rebut this presumption. Understandably so, since one would assume that people in business anticipated their transactions to have legal consequences.

But if you are in business and you really do not want a

particular transaction to have legal consequences, declare it expressly and the court will hardly be able to find otherwise. Many of us each week enter into a transaction with a major business concern under which we pay over money and cheerfully sign away our legal right to hold the other party to his promises. Maybe you are one of the millions of people who enter the football pools. Next time you fill in your pools coupon, check the wording at the bottom and you will almost certainly find an expression along the lines, 'this agreement is binding in honour only'. The courts have held such an expression to mean that the parties do not intend the transaction to amount to a legally binding agreement. In a famous case, the plaintiff (the one who brings the case), Mr Jones, claimed he had eight score draws, but the pools company refused to pay out on the basis that they did not have the coupon. He didn't get his money.

Consideration

You will recall that, in this context, consideration is a legal term denoting the third essential ingredient of a contract.

We can best explain its meaning by the following example. A generous uncle has a favourite nephew and next week it is the nephew's 21st birthday. The uncle goes to his nephew and says, 'You've always been my favourite and it's your birthday next week. I've just bought a brand new car and I'm going to give you my other one on your birthday. I'll be round next week with my one-year-old GLX.'

The nephew is overwhelmed. 'I can't let you do that,' he responds. The uncle insists. 'You're my favourite. I'll bring it round next Wednesday.' Naturally the nephew is thrilled and excited.

Next Wednesday the uncle does not turn up. The gleaming GLX remains but a dream, uncle unable to resist a tempting offer for it.

The dejected nephew has no legal redress. He cannot sue his uncle for breach of contract, because all uncle has done was to promise to make a gift, and (subject to one exception we shall look at later) English law does not enforce promises to make a gift.

However, it might have been very different if the conversation had gone like this. If the nephew had said to his uncle: 'I can't let you give it to me. But I've got £500 saved up in the building society – the car's worth a lot more, but at least take that to ease my conscience.'

Had the uncle agreed and promised to let his nephew have the car for £500, the gift may have been transformed into a contract of sale. This time, if the car had not been delivered on Wednesday, the nephew might have had the right to sue the uncle for breach of contract. We say 'might' because of course, we have to bear in mind the need for intention to create legal relations, which the court might not feel was present here where the parties were related. That apart, the key difference is that in the alternative scenario not only was the nephew getting something from the uncle, the uncle was also getting something from the nephew. It was a two-way transaction, something moving from one party to the other, and vice versa.

Consideration then is this: in order to show that the agreement is a contract, you must prove that the other party is receiving something back from you in return.

It is not necessary to show that the other party actually received that something; the *promise* to deliver the car is consideration. Commonly, in fact, the consideration that both parties give takes the form of a promise, eg *S* promises to deliver the car on Wednesday, *B* promises to pay £500 for it on delivery.

Our definition of consideration is rather wide and needs some pruning back. The courts do not take the view that anything taken can make an agreement binding. What the courts say is that for something to be recognised as consideration it must be *valuable*.

Again we meet a commonplace word which has a different meaning in legal circles from that in everyday speech. In daily life we use the word to speak of a valuable antique or a valuable painting, employing it to denote great value.

For the law to recognise something as consideration you must be able to value it. It must have some value – not necessarily great value, but some. By this we mean some monetary or economic value as opposed to, for example, merely sentimental value. So consideration may come in the form of goods or services or, of course, money itself.

The law will, though, recognise something quite insignificant as constituting consideration. Some item of tiny value, such as a box of matches or a copy of yesterday's newspaper could be valuable consideration.

So, in the eyes of the law, could an agreement be enforced to exchange a box of matches for, say, a pair of silver candlesticks? Surely the court will say that the consideration given is not good enough?

The court will not. In its heart English law has always taken the view that it is for the parties to make their own deal. If one of the parties chooses for his own reasons to sell for £5 an object with a market value of £500 that is his choice. The law gives you a set of rules by which you must abide if you want your agreement to be legally binding; as long as you follow them, the court will hold you to the agreement. Of course the law has for centuries recognised the need to protect those who are unable to look after their own interests, such as children. But even today it behoves contracting parties to bear in mind the law's maxim *caveat emptor*, latin for 'buyer beware'. Give consideration, even if what you get back is far less valuable than what you receive, and you make a contract – not forgetting intention and agreement of course.

If the court upholds an agreement to sell an object worth £500 for £5, this would be an example of nominal consideration, an expression most of us have heard used at some time. So if your uncle comes to you and says, 'I'm planning to give you a brand new Porsche', show him some *legal* consideration. Say, 'Oh no, I can't let you do that. But why not let me come and baby-sit for you on Saturday night . . . ?'

Everyday contracts

We have said that each of us probably makes several agreements every day, dozens every week. You will have realised by now that many of these agreements are contracts: that we make hundreds of contracts in our personal and professional lives during the course of a year. At work we make a contract for the firm when we buy stationery, put petrol in the firm's van, buy in stock, take on a new cleaner, lease a replacement photocopier. We make a contract for ourselves every time we buy a newspaper, get on a bus, have a meal out, have a haircut, go to the supermarket, have the windows cleaned, have a drink in the local. The law of contract is about everyday transactions, in both personal and business life.

At this point, you may be thinking that while the little everyday transactions are contracts in legal theory, they are not important; that those of consequence are the ones most people think of as contracts – when we sign to buy a car on credit, or the firm leases a new computer.

But what happens if those little everyday transactions *go wrong*? If the plumber makes a bodge-up of installing your dishwasher or if the pair of underpants you bought for £1.95 give you a horrible disease?

It could be a *breach of contract*. You could have the right to sue because someone agreed to do something and failed to keep to the agreement. The plumber made a contract to install a dishwasher, exercising reasonable skill and care, so that it would function. He did not undertake to install a dishwasher that leaks water out of the back. The seller made a contract to supply you with a pair of underpants fit for the purpose of wearing, not a pair of *dangerous* underpants. Incidentally, if you think the latter is a somewhat far-fetched illustration, that is exactly what happened to a Mr Grant in a real case.

Solicitors will tell you that most of their clients think that just because they have suffered harm, they must under the law have the right to sue somebody. This is not so. The law has to allow all of us to suffer harm from time to time without legal redress.

Let us suppose you own a corner grocery shop, and a giant supermarket opens up next door. They are able to undercut your prices, your trade falls off to an unprofitable level, and you are forced to close down. You cannot sue your competitor. Our society takes the view that free competition is on the whole in everybody's interest, even though some individuals will suffer in the process. You cannot show that a *legal wrong* has been done to you.

Probably the simplest way to prove that you or your business has suffered a *legal* wrong is to show you made a contract – a legally binding agreement – and it has been broken.

Sometimes you may be able to show that what has happened amounts to more than one legal wrong done to you, since the law gives us all a number of legal rights. For example, someone has failed to take reasonable care when they should have done, or someone is in breach of consumer protection laws. But perhaps you cannot actually prove that the other party failed to take reasonable care, or what occurred was in the course of your business and so you are not 'a consumer' in the eyes of the law. But if you can simply show that someone undertook to do something in return for a consideration, and they have not done it . . .

Probably the biggest weapon you can take up in the legal armoury is the sword of contract.

Summary

- A contract is an agreement that is legally binding.
- For an agreement to be legally binding it must have three essential elements: agreement, intention, consideration.
- In deciding whether there was agreement the usual approach of the courts is to look for an offer made by one party and an acceptance made by the other.
- An intention that the agreement was to be legally binding will be presumed in commercial transactions, until the contrary can be shown.
- The party seeking to enforce the agreement must show that the other party was receiving something back in return for agreeing.

Chapter 3

The Forms a Contract May Take

It is a common misconception, even in the world of business, that the word contract denotes only a formal written document. In fact our introductory survey of the law of contract shows that a contract may take a number of forms.

This chapter examines the main alternative forms of contract, pointing out some of the particular problems of each, and some of the considerations that should be taken into account in deciding whether to allow a transaction to take a particular form. In the overwhelming majority of cases the law allows us to choose the form a contract will take. Usually there is no legal requirement that the contract shall, for example, be in writing or, if it is a written document, be set out in a particular manner. There are, however, some important exceptions to this, including contracts involving land and buildings (what lawyers call real property) and contracts granting credit to a consumer.

A contract may take one of the following forms:

- an oral agreement;
- an agreement partly oral and partly in writing;
- an agreement in writing;
- an agreement inferred from conduct;
- a deed.

These are broad categorisations and the second and third in particular each embrace an array of contract sub-species.

Oral contracts

Many commonplace transactions may appear at first glance to be purely oral agreements; but in practice on closer examination often these agreements also embrace something in writing. The window cleaner calling upon a domestic householder may agree all his needs with his customers orally, but the dry cleaning shop will almost certainly attempt to incorporate some terms into the transaction with its customer other than what passes between the parties by word of mouth: for example, a notice displayed in the premises. In practice, transactions where both the parties are in business are even less likely to be purely oral.

The main question concerning oral agreements is: how do you prove it? The answer is that going to court and testifying in the witness box as to what was said is, of course, evidence. This usually prompts another question: 'But if it is simply my word against his, then where are we?'

It rests on the decision of whose testimony the judge prefers. The judge will weigh up the quality of the testimony. Are you a witness who tells the truth? Are you a person of good character? If both parties are credible and there is no other evidence in support, the approach of the courts is that it is for the one who brings the case (the plaintiff) to prove it. To do this he only needs to tip the scales sufficiently for the judge to feel that, on balance, the probability is that matters are as he asserts; but if the evidence is 50/50, the plaintiff has not proved his case and must lose.

Contracts partly oral and partly written

The example of the dry cleaning business shows that the written element of a partly oral and partly written contract may be found on pieces of paper which consumers, bearing in mind what they think a contract is, might not expect to contain the terms of a contract. In practice, the courts often have to collect together the agreement from things said by the parties, letters passing between them, notices displayed, statements in business literature such as catalogues and price lists, and documentation such as order forms.

In some transactions which would otherwise be by word of mouth, the company may have good reason to incorporate a particular term in writing. It may be too important to run the risk of the company's staff omitting to state it orally. In the example of the high street dry cleaners, the business may wish to make it clear that it cannot accept liability for, say, damage to the sequins on a dress. Instead of leaving it to the assistant to remember to say this to the customer on every occasion, in practice the shop will display a notice for the customer to see, or put a clause on the customer's receipt, or possibly even prepare a leaflet, setting out the shop's position, to be handed to the customer.

With all these strategies, there is a danger for the business that the clause will not be viewed by the court as part of the contract, and therefore not binding on the other party. The same problem arises in the case of invoices and delivery notes which purport to include contractual terms. The process of offer and acceptance that we looked at earlier shows us how the problem can arise. We have seen that the agreement is concluded when an acceptance is made known to the party who made the offer. Therefore if a document or notice would not come to the attention of the other party before they make acceptance, then they cannot be said to have agreed to it.

In the case of a clause set out in a receipt or an invoice, how can it be said to have been brought to the notice of the other party before the agreement was concluded, since both these documents are required *because* an agreement has been concluded?

Olley v Marlborough Court Hotel (1949)

The plaintiff and her husband appeared at the defendant's hotel and made arrangements for seven days' accommodation. After making the arrangements they went up to their allotted bedroom, on one wall of which was displayed a notice purporting to exclude the hotel's liability for guests' articles unless handed to the manageress for custody.

The court held that the contract was completed before the guests went up to the room and the clause was not a part of the agreement.

How can you ensure that, in what would otherwise be an oral contract, an important clause is made a part of the agreement? In the example of the dry cleaners the shop can display a notice, but it must be sufficiently prominent for a reasonable person to have noticed and read the clause *before* agreeing the transaction. Or the assistant can hand over a leaflet to the customer setting out the clause but, again, it must be before the customer agrees the transaction.

As we have seen, the test to decide whether the parties agreed to something is: would a reasonable bystander think they agreed? Thus it is not usually necessary to prove that the other party was *actually* aware of the term. After all, the other party may not have seen the clause because of their own lack of care. This does not mean that one party to a contract can record a term on any old piece of paper regardless of whether the other party is likely to read it. In the example of the dry cleaners, if a clause were to be written on a cigarette packet left lying on the counter, the court would not take the view that this was incorporated into the contract! For the clause to be part of the contract it must be contained in a document which a reasonable person would expect to contain a contractual clause. In one case, deck chairs for hire at a seaside resort were stacked alongside a notice stating the cost of the hire. The notice requested the public to obtain tickets from an attendant and to retain the tickets for inspection. The plaintiff took two chairs, obtained the tickets from the attendant, and put them in his pocket. He was injured when one of the chairs collapsed. The defendants claimed they had excluded their liability for such a mishap by a provision printed on the ticket. The court said that a reasonable person would think the ticket was only a receipt for the money paid and not a document containing contractual terms, and the plaintiff succeeded.

This is not to say that a ticket is incapable of containing a contractual term or referring to terms set out elsewhere which can be read by the holder of the ticket. Remember, the test is what would a reasonable person think in the particular circumstances? The reasonable person knows, for example, that a railway or bus ticket refers to terms of the contract of carriage.

There is also the problem that provisions on a ticket have probably been introduced after the agreement has been made (similarly with invoices). There is one way of saving the situation. The parties may have had previous dealings in which the post-agreement document, with the clause, was supplied to the other party. Where there are such dealings the court may say this fixes the other party with knowledge of the clause. However, putting clauses on a post-agreement document and then relying on the court taking this view is clearly not to be recommended. It seems there must have been regular dealings between the parties, whereas the transaction may prove to be a one-off or the dealings between the parties spasmodic.

> *Troubleshooting. Is your business attempting to include terms after the contract has been made? Are you putting terms on an invoice, a delivery note, or other post-agreement document?*

Contracts in writing

For most non-lawyers the expression 'contract in writing' conjures up a typed or printed document, formally worded and signed by the parties.

In practice, the commonest type of contract in writing is to be found in printed documentation issued by businesses to regulate their relationship with customers or suppliers. The document might describe itself as a Contract or an Agreement or, possibly, as an Order Form or a

Quotation. It might not be a single document. Perhaps two, or even more, together constitute the written contract.

Sometimes what the parties may regard as a written contract is, in truth, one which is partly written and partly oral; for example, where the standard documentation only sets out part of what has to be agreed. Whether the agreement truly is a 'contract in writing' does matter. In the event of a dispute, neither of the parties can attempt to add on to the written contract oral clauses allegedly also agreed. If the court takes the view that the parties intended the written document to set out their agreement – a true 'written contract' – then the parties will not be able to bring evidence of oral exchanges that add to it, vary it or contradict it. The reasoning behind this is that the primary purpose of a written contract is to give certainty to the understanding of the parties. If the parties intended to have a written contract, it is not for the court to defeat their intention. But did they intend the contract to be wholly in writing or did they intend it to be partly written and partly oral?

This is for the court to decide. In practice, in a particular case, to exclude something that passed between the parties orally often strikes the court as being unjust. In such a case the court is likely either to find that the contract was not intended to be solely in writing, or use a device known as the 'collateral contract'. Here, although the parties have an agreement in writing, the court takes the view that oral arrangements also made constitute a second, separate contract. Very often the oral statement was some undertaking given to the other side to induce them to enter into the written contract.

Some businesses make it a practice to include in their documentation a clause reciting that the document contains *all* the terms of the agreement between the parties. There appears to be no reported case on the effectiveness of such an attempt to keep out the possibility of orally adding to or varying the standard terms. Where a court felt constrained by the interests of justice, it might still find a way to lift its eyes from the written document.

Deeds

A written contract can take the form of a *deed*. This is the most elaborate and formal method of making a contract in which not only is the agreement in writing but it is also signed and witnessed. A contract made in the form of a deed is commonly referred to as a contract under seal. In former times this involved affixing a wax seal to the document, which was later replaced by self-adhesive paper seals bought by solicitors from the stationers. The requirement for a seal of any sort has recently been abolished.

One reason for going through the formalities of making the deed is that a contract made in this way does not require consideration. Since commonplace business transactions usually involve both sides giving consideration, the use of the deed to make such a contract is unnecessary in daily business life, although in a few trades it is still the custom for contracts to be made in this form. A promise to make a gift would be legally binding if a deed was used; without one it would not be, because by definition, no consideration is given by the recipient.

Letters

Written contracts often take the form of an exchange of correspondence. A consequence of dealing by post is that one of the parties is likely to become bound by a contract which comes into being before he is aware of it.

We have seen earlier that a contract comes into being and the parties are bound at the stage when an acceptance is made known to the party who made the offer. Where an acceptance of an offer takes the form of a letter, the acceptance will be deemed to be communicated – and the contract come into being and the parties thus bound – from the time that the letter of acceptance is put into the post. The law does not wait for it to be opened or even delivered before it is deemed to be communicated. Unless the party to whom the letter is sent is otherwise made aware of the acceptance, while it is in the post they will be bound by an agreement not knowing that it has come into existence.

It is not necessary for the party receiving the acceptance to have made the offer by post. The rule – known to judges and lawyers as 'the post rule' – applies provided it is reasonable for the other party to use the post. Thus in one case an offer was made in a written note handed to the plaintiff, who replied accepting by letter posted the next day. The court held the parties were bound when the letter of acceptance was posted.

What happens if the letter of acceptance is lost in the post and never received? Surely the offeror will not be bound by a contract of whose existence he did not know?

Household Fire Insurance Co Ltd v Grant (1879)

The defendant made an offer to buy shares in the plaintiff company. The company secretary posted a letter of acceptance to the defendant. The letter never arrived. The company then went into liquidation and payment was claimed for the shares.

The Court of Appeal held that the contract to buy shares was complete, final and binding as soon as the acceptance letter was posted. The defendant must pay for the shares.

Once we are alerted to the danger inherent in the posting rule, provision can be made for it. The judges have said that the operation of the rule can be ousted by a condition laid down in making the offer. Thus an agreement that has been drafted by a lawyer often contains a clause to the effect that the agreement will not come into being until the party who made the offer actually receives notification of acceptance.

Stipulating how acceptance should be made

Going one stage further, it has become increasingly common in recent years for one of the parties to stipulate that the other must make their acceptance in a particular way. The lawyers call this prescribing the mode of acceptance. Perhaps, for example, one of the parties stipulates that acceptance must be made on a particular document supplied by that party.

The layperson might think that if the other party fails to comply with this condition, there would not be a valid acceptance. The courts have not, however, taken this simple line and in modern cases have said that an acceptance in some other manner will still be valid provided the other party is put in no worse a position by this deviation.

Yates Building v Pulleyn & Sons (1975)

An offer was made by the defendants to sell the plaintiffs a plot of land. If they wished to accept the offer the plaintiffs were to give notice in writing 'sent by registered or recorded delivery'. The plaintiffs sent their letter by ordinary post. The defendants contended this was not a valid acceptance. *The Court of Appeal held* that the offer was validly accepted.

Accordingly, if the offeror wishes to lay down the manner in which the other party is to accept and assure compliance, he should recite that this mode only will suffice and that no other method of acceptance will create a valid agreement.

Communications by telex and fax

The rule that a letter of acceptance is deemed to be communicated when it is put into the post is an exception to the general rule that acceptance must be made known to the party who made the offer. This exception does not apply to communications made by telex. It has been held that notification of acceptance sent by telex is not binding until it is received on the telex equipment of the party who made the offer.

It seems quite likely that the courts will take a similar view of communications made via fax, and will hold that there is no binding contract until notice of the acceptance is received on the offeror's fax machine.

Letters of intent

We saw in our introduction to contract law in Chapter 1 how, to determine whether an agreement has been made, usually the court looks to see if one party made an offer, which was then accepted by the other. An offer, it will be recalled, is a statement of terms which it appears you are willing to stand by.

An offer must be distinguished from a statement of intention: a statement informing someone of what you intend to do in the future. This is not capable of being 'accepted' and thus forming a contract. For example, a firm of auctioneers placed notices in the newspaper announcing that they were to hold an auction of office furniture at Bury St Edmunds in Suffolk. A prospective bidder saw the announcement of the auction and travelled to Bury on the auction date. The auction was cancelled. The prospective buyer sued the auctioners for compensation for his fruitless journey. The court said the notices were an announcement of the auctioneers' intention to hold an auction, not an offer to do so which had been accepted by the plaintiff turning up at the auction venue. The auctioneers, in merely stating their intention, were entitled to change their mind.

Sometimes a party may wish to make known their intention to enter into a contract. One business may, for example, be involved with another in negotiations which cannot yet, for various reasons, be concluded; but one of the parties wishes the other to understand that it is their intention to enter into a contract. In certain industries where subcontractors are used to enable a party to carry out a large-scale undertaking, such as building and civil engineering, it is a common practice to write letters of intent. The party concerned may not yet have secured the main contract and therefore cannot bind himself to subcontracts, but wishes a proposed subcontractor to know that it is his intention to contract with him when he is able to do so.

There is no reason why such a letter of intent, if *properly drafted*, should give rise to legal liability. Sometimes, however, although the parties cannot yet conclude negotiations, the party sending the letter of intent wishes the other to commence work under the proposed contract so as to avoid delays while the final details of the contract are worked out. In this situation, when the negotiations are concluded and the contract formed, that work will be covered by the contract. Thus, if the party who has had the work done refused to pay for it they could be sued for breach of contract, and the contract price recovered for that work, together with any other compensation due for breach. Likewise, if the party carrying out the work wrongfully refuses to complete it, he will be liable for breach – because there is a contract in existence, the normal consequences arise, including liability for breach of that contract. If one party commences work while negotiations are still in hand and the deal then falls through, there is no contract, so that party cannot sue for payment under the contract.

There are a number of situations that can arise in business and personal life where one person receives something from another and it would be wrong to allow the recipient to have the benefit without making some payment for it. In such circumstances justice demands that the recipient pays a reasonable sum for what has been received. Where the negotiations do not result in a contract, the prospective contractor can recover a reasonable sum for the work he was asked to carry out in contemplation of the contract; he can recover on what lawyers call a *quantum meruit* basis. Of course, the sum recovered on this basis may be considerably less than what he would have received under the contract had there been one. On the other hand, he cannot be required to finish the work, since he has no contractual obligation to do so.

Tenders

The process of tendering is a common practice with public bodies such as local authorities and government departments, and in some particular industries, such as building. We all see advertisements in newspapers for tenders for the supply or purchase of goods: an announcement by auctioneers inviting tenders to buy cars or other items seized by the courts from debtors is an eye-catching example. The usual practice is to ask for 'tenders in writing', although as a matter of law there is no need for this.

Business people who are unfamiliar with the process of tendering may be put off trying to get business in this way. They feel it is a specialised form of contracting about which they have no knowledge and in which there lurks unknown pitfalls. In fact, an advertisement inviting tenders is inviting people to make *offers*.

You may ask: 'If I put in a tender and it is accepted, am I bound by it?' The answer depends, of course, on what the parties have agreed, which in turn depends on what was stated in the invitation to make tenders. It may well be that 'acceptance' of the tender has created a contractual obligation. If, for example, the invitation was to tender for the supply of specific goods, eg 'three ambulances', then by accepting the tender that party is bound to take and pay for the goods and the tenderer is bound to supply them.

Tenders are often used where the party concerned is seeking supplies over a given period. Tenders for '12,000 gallons of heating oil to be supplied and delivered at the rate of 1000 gallons per calendar month during the year 1992' will, if accepted, create a contract to supply and take the goods in the manner provided. But where the buyer is seeking supplies over a period of time he may not be sure what quantity he will require or even if he will require any supplies at all during that period. Thus the invitation may invite tenders to supply goods the party 'may' require and 'if' demanded. This does not create an obligation on the buyer to take goods, unless and until he does requisition some. The tenderer makes a *standing offer* and if and when the buyer requisitions the goods, this amounts to an acceptance of an offer. Each and any subsequent requisitions create a separate contract.

By inviting tenders the party is inviting offers which he is free to accept or reject, unless he has stated that he *will* accept the lowest offer to supply (or highest offer to buy, as the case may be). However, a recent decision of the Court of Appeal has broken new ground in the field of tenders. The court held that in certain circumstances by inviting others to go to the trouble of complying with the procedure and conditions laid down for the submission of tenders, the party inviting the tenders may be putting himself under an obligation at least to *consider* a tender submitted; although he may then come to a bona fide decision to reject the tender.

Standard form contracts

It is common practice for businesses to use their own standard printed documentation in dealings with customers and, to a lesser extent, suppliers. The agreements contained in these documents have become known as standard form contracts. One party is offering the same standard terms to different contracting partners.

Some businesses offer standard terms which are fair and reasonable to both parties, but it is more likely that a business will attempt to draw up terms which are, to varying degrees, one-sidedly in their favour.

Standard form documentation has become so popular in recent years that it is now commonplace for two businesses to find that they are each attempting to deal on their own standard terms which, of course, will not be identical. This has become known as the battle of the forms – each business endeavouring to conclude the agreement on its own terms. It can lead to the most determined battle of wills, with each party insisting that their terms will prevail. However, in other offices up and down the land, personnel, unaware of the legal position, allow the other party's documentation to pass through their procedures without realising what they are doing: contracting on the other party's terms.

From the supplier's point of view, it is quite common to provide an order form, incorporating his terms, for completion, signature and return by the buyer. The use of order forms, which may be viewed by many buyers as a convenience, is often made without giving the matter further thought. In this way the contract can be concluded on the supplier's terms.

The buyer can provide a form for the supplier to insert a quotation, sign and return, so that the contract will be on the buyer's terms. Such forms are not so common generally in business as order forms and there may be a greater reluctance on the part of the recipient to complete the form. Indeed, it is often the provision of this type of form by the buyer that trumpets a forthcoming battle of the forms.

If a dispute subsequently arises between the parties, undoubtedly each side will turn to their printed terms. The question is: whose terms apply? Where the parties have entered into a transaction without sorting out on whose terms they are proceeding, or there has been a battle of the forms, the judge will have to decide whose terms governed the deal; not all judges and arbitrators have adopted the same approach when sorting out the mess.

One of the devices used by some companies in an attempt to ensure that their own terms prevail, is to include in their documentation a printed acknowledgement that they require the other side to complete. This will usually state that the agreement has been made on the terms of the party to whom the acknowledgement is being returned.

Faced with a battle of the forms, the judges have tended to fall back on fundamental principles of contract law, applying the rules of offer and acceptance that we looked at in Chapter 1, analysing events into a process of offers and *counter offers*.

Counter offers

One party makes an offer. The other party then comes back with a variation of that offer, the counter offer. Counter offers, which can be either oral or written, are a feature of daily business life, yet the making of a counter offer has huge impact in the eyes of the law.

First, where one of the parties replies with a counter offer, it is as if he had said no to the original offer; the courts have held that the effect of making a counter offer is to reject the original. Second, the effect of a refusal – and this applies whether it is in the form of a counter offer or a simple 'no' – is to destroy the original offer. This means that the original offer is no longer in existence should the party making the counter offer find that it is not acceptable and then wish to accept the original offer.

In the ordinary course of events the party who made the original offer will be only too pleased to proceed on his original terms; the point is that he does not *have* to do so. The party may have made an offer with which he now does not wish to proceed. Such a change of mind could occur very rapidly in a world where there are sudden price changes, for example when dealing with commodities or shares in companies. It may have suited the offeror to have made an offer of x tonnes of coffee at y price five minutes ago, but the price of coffee having risen on the market in the meantime, it would now be more profitable for him to seek a deal elsewhere.

The battle of the forms

Where the court adopts the approach of analysing events into a process of offers and counter offers, the contract will be held to have been made on the terms of the party whose final counter offer was accepted. The following example may make this clearer.

Buyer Ltd places an order on its standard documentation stating that the order is to be on its terms. Supplier Ltd replies 'accepting' the order but stating that the sale is to be on Supplier's terms. Here the court would likely take the view that the placing of the order constituted an offer and the purported acceptance by Supplier was a counter offer, the effect of which was to reject the offer. At this stage it is possible that someone at Buyer Ltd will pick up Supplier's reply and respond that this is unacceptable, at which time no concluded agreement has been made.

What is the position, however, if Buyer Ltd allowed the transaction to proceed without challenging Supplier's purported acceptance? Supplier makes delivery of the goods. If Buyer were then to accept such delivery it is likely that the court would conclude that by doing so Buyer has accepted Supplier's counter offer. No doubt in the real world, as the employees of Buyer take delivery, they are not aware that they are making acceptance of a counter offer. It will be recalled, however, that the test of whether or not the parties made an agreement is: does it *look* as if the parties made an agreement? The court might say that Buyer's acceptance of Supplier's counter offer could be inferred from their act of taking delivery of the goods.

This takes us right back to the very basics of contract: while most lay persons probably take the view that to make a legally binding agreement it is necessary to have a formal written document, the legal reality is that an agreement can be made between persons who do not even speak, let alone write. Both an offer to make a contract and its acceptance can be implied from conduct. If, for example, a customer in a self-service store removes an item from the display and presents it at the check-out, and the assistant rings up the price on the till and accepts the money without either party speaking, undoubtedly a valid contract has been made.

Butler Machine Tool Co v Ex Cell O Corporation (1979)

The plaintiffs offered to supply a machine tool, the quotation being made on their standard printed stationery. The terms of supply included a clause entitling them to charge the price ruling at the time of delivery, which was to be some ten months later, rather than at the date of ordering.

The buyers placed an order using their own standard order documentation, the terms of which did not provide for the price to be varied. This documentation included a tear-off slip for their suppliers to return, which the plaintiffs did, the slip acknowledging that the order was accepted on the terms set out in the buyer's documentation.

By the time of delivery the price had increased by £2800, which the buyers refused to pay.

The Court of Appeal held that the contract had been made on the buyers' terms, their order documentation constituting a counter offer, rejecting the suppliers' terms. This counter offer had been accepted by the suppliers when they returned that acknowledgement slip.

A lesson to be drawn from the Butler case is that staff should read and consider carefully documentation emanating from the other side before returning it. Such elementary advice may be thought to be stating the obvious, but whereas staff would be hesitant to return a typewritten document of formal appearance bearing the heading 'Contract', they may not realise the significance of returning a tear-off printed slip in acknowledgement. The individual member of staff concerned would feel he was being businesslike or polite. In fact he might have committed a gross tactical error in the battle of the forms, upon which a subsequent legal war could turn!

Variation of the contract

Troubleshooting. Do members of staff agree to variations asked for by contracting parties, varying the other party's obligations under your carefully worded agreements?

Having succeeded in making the contract on your own terms, you will wish to try and guard against it being varied subsequently for the benefit of the other party. In practice, a member of your staff might later on agree to a concession asked for by the other party; for example, a request to deliver later than provided for in the contract. Because the other side are bound to perform their obligations, they cannot unilaterally elect not to do so – that would be breach of the contract – so they may, for example, ring up and ask someone if it is okay to do *XYZ* instead of *ABC*.

In this situation you will see that the other side is seeking your agreement to something; technically, therefore, to make your agreement to their proposal binding, the other side should provide consideration. If what they suggest could also be of benefit to your business, then there may be consideration and your agreement to the change is therefore binding. For example, in a contract for the purchase of goods the terms provide for payment by you 28 days after delivery. By agreeing to the other side delaying delivery you also delay the date when payment is due from you, which is of benefit to you. Even without the other side giving consideration for you agreeing to a variation, in some circumstances the court may hold you to the variation if the other side have relied on the fact that you agreed and then acted on it.

In order to guard against a member of staff, who might have the apparent authority, agreeing a variation of the terms, it is quite common to insert in a standard form contract a clause along the lines that no variation of the terms will be binding unless agreed in writing by an official of specified seniority, for example, a director. This might at least deter the other side from attempting to get agreement to a concession from a member of staff.

Chapter 4

Written Contracts

Although the general rule is that an agreement does not have to be in writing to be binding, there are compelling reasons for putting your agreements in written form.

Millions of transactions take place daily where it would be wholly inappropriate to have a written document, mainly because the parties would regard the matter as being too trivial to warrant a formal, written agreement. The customer who pops into the sweet shop to buy a packet of mints will hesitate if he finds he has to sign an agreement before rushing off to catch his bus. But even this commonplace transaction involving a tiny sum of money is a reminder that some of what the parties have agreed may appear in writing somewhere, though not in a formal written document. In this example there will be some text emblazoned on the wrapper in such a way that the buyer sees it when making his choice. The description 'extra strong mints' will be part of the terms of the contract.

A great number of small, and not so small organisations are quite happy to bump along doing business leaving some if not all of the matters they agreed to the parties' recall of what was said and – just as important – what was left unsaid. Perhaps the court will have to collect together the contract from a telephone conversation, a comment made by a member of staff to the customer in the workshop, a letter, a notice displayed in reception, and a page torn from a duplicate book headed 'Order' or 'Quotation'. Such a business is presumably unaware of the benefits of:

(a) devising, where appropriate, its own set of terms upon which it will do business, or

(b) if possible, using its own comprehensive standard form document, embodying the terms, that constitutes a signed written contract.

The advantages of a set of terms

There are many advantages for the business which uses its own standard set of terms.

1. By spelling out what both parties are to receive – and their respective obligations – you can avoid customer disappointment. It can also nip in the bud some potential disputes by enabling you to point a finger at what is stated in writing.

2. We have seen that it may be desirable and possible to oust some of the rules provided by contract law – for example, that a contract comes into being when a letter of acceptance is put into the post. The use of standard form terms which include an appropriate clause would achieve this as a matter of practice.

3. A set of written terms can anticipate contingencies and make provision for them. Events can occur which would make the carrying out of the contract more difficult but, because they are unlikely, the parties have not given attention to them. Unlikely problems *will* occur if there are sufficient numbers of transactions. By providing a set of terms for all transactions you will avoid those unfortunate situations.

4. The set of terms can be drafted so that they are favourable to the interests of your business.

    The extent to which you can tilt an agreement in your favour is of course influenced by commercial considerations: would this be acceptable to the other party, be they customer or supplier? In turn this will depend upon your relative bargaining position. If you are fortunate enough to be Big Household Name Ltd with a choice of eager suppliers, then you may be able to dictate strict terms with which the other party will struggle to comply. If the situation is reversed however . . .

    Some household name companies have an unenviable reputation for using their bargaining strength to impose terms on suppliers which are almost Draconian. There are always some suppliers who will subject themselves to dictatorial terms in order to get the business. Perhaps the dictator companies should ask themselves whether they are making commercial life unnecessarily difficult for both parties. Suppliers are human and if they are resentful in their dealings with Mr Big, are they really likely to give of their best, or create the most favourable relationship? It may better suit your business interests to draft an agreement which fairly balances the interests of both parties, thus helping to avoid ill feeling in the other. This is not to say that the opportunity should be missed to safeguard yourself fully against the occasional customer/supplier who might let you down. Apart from making provision to avoid the more obvious things such as failure to pay or inability to supply, try to recall problems that have arisen in your own business and see whether you can safeguard against them in the written agreement.

5. By inserting an *effective* clause you can limit your legal liability, or perhaps exclude liability altogether in certain circumstances. We emphasise effective, because the courts are not eager to find that a notice, ticket etc containing such a clause – usually referred to as an exclusion clause – is a part of the contract. Exclusion clauses also need special care in their drafting as they are interpreted strictly by the courts, not unnaturally. Such clauses are attempting to allow the party concerned to escape liability, for example because he has failed to do what he promised under the agreement, so any ambiguity will be resolved against the party seeking to rely on it. In some reported cases the court appears to have strained itself to find ambiguity! That said, the courts' attitudes towards such exclusion clauses seem to have softened slightly in recent years, since Parliament intervened with the passing of the *Unfair Contract Terms Act 1977*. Before the Act, the use of such clauses sometimes had scandalous results, allowing one side to ride free after imposing considerable harm on the other party.

   In business, however, there are circumstances in which it will be legitimate to include a clause which attempts to limit or even exclude liability. Their use is also more acceptable where the other party has a choice in the matter. An example of a justifiable clause would be where the existence of the clause enables you to offer a lower price than a competitor who is prepared to run the risk of accepting greater liability. In these circumstances the customer has a choice: he can elect whether or not to pay more and enjoy greater cover against things going wrong. There is no reason why an exclusion clause should not be an example of 'you get what you pay for'.

   We shall be returning to exclusion clauses later when we consider the contents of your contract and will see then that in certain types of contract Parliament has placed severe restrictions on the extent to which one party can shield itself behind an exclusion clause, and in some cases has prohibited this altogether.

   An exclusion clause is an excellent example of just the sort of provision that should not be made up as you dictate a letter to the other side!

6.   You can take the opportunity to leave out clauses that the law would otherwise insert into the agreement for you.

The majority of everyday contracts involves the sale of goods, for which the law provides a ready-made collection of terms and rules governing the rights of the parties. Indeed, you could use these rules to provide the contents of almost the whole contract if you so wish, including the price! These terms are set out in the *Sale of Goods Act 1979*. (They do not, incidentally, apply to leasing contracts, under which the goods are used by the customer but there is no transfer of ownership – no sale of goods – to him.)

The law also puts some terms into a contract for the supply of services: that is to say, one where a party is to perform work under the contract. These are found in the *Supply of Goods and Services Act 1982*, but the Act only deals with the essential matters such as price and quality, and does not provide the extensive framework set out in the Sale of Goods Act.

Note well: if you do not make provision yourself for the matters covered by the Acts, eg when ownership is to pass and when delivery is to be made, and the Act settles these matters for you, you may find that what the law has provided is not what you would have agreed had you thought about it. In the case of the sale of goods, the terms and rules provided by the Act may be particularly inappropriate for certain trades and industries. This is because, although the Act was passed in 1979, it is based upon one passed in 1893 that was subsequently amended over the years. The objective of the 1979 Act was to set out the old law including all its amendments; it is really a nineteenth century statute applying a framework and a code that is 100 years old. Commentators have pointed out that since the original Act was passed we have witnessed revolutionary technical and commercial changes. The Act may not make appropriate provision for industries that have arisen since then, in particular hi-tech industries. Are the terms and rules provided by the Act suitable for your particular trade?

The practice of inserting terms into your contract is not limited to Parliament's intervention. In some types of contract the judges have taken it upon themselves to insert terms, with a view to building up what the famous judge Lord Denning called a paradigm contract. Here the courts are putting together an example contract, inserting terms for no better reason than that they consider it reasonable for a contract of the type in question to have such a term. Fortunately this has been confined to very few types of contract, the most important being contracts of employment and contracts involving land and buildings.

Finally, sometimes the courts will declare a term to be existing in a contract to reflect a custom or practice of a particular trade.

You may feel it is better to make express provision for your own particular trade, your own particular business, and your own particular methods of business, than to leave matters to these various sources.

Incorporating a set of terms

As we have observed earlier, it is simply not commercially or logistically viable in some businesses to attempt to get the other party to sign a written contract, nor even to present them with a set of written terms. Yet the nature of the business, the complexity or scale of its operations for example, may demand a set of terms to cover those operations. A good example of this is the railways. It is not a practical proposition to hand a complete set of the terms under which British Rail does business to every passenger every time they buy a ticket.

How, in these circumstances, are the terms to be incorporated into the contract? We have met the problem before (see Chapter 3, pp. 27–9), where we saw that you must show you made reasonable efforts to bring the terms to the attention of the other party. It is why we see notices or tickets declaring that the transaction is 'subject to the company's terms of business, a copy of which can be had on request', or something similar. Whether or not such an attempt to incorporate a set of terms is successful depends on the view of the court's friend, the reasonable person. Would the fact that there was a set of terms in existence have become known to the reasonable person? The answer to this question will be 'no' where the reasonable person would not have seen the notice, for example, because it was not big enough or had fallen down or had been moved. In some circumstances the reasonable person would *know* even without the efforts of the other party that there must be a set of terms governing the transaction, because it is common knowledge; travelling on the railway would again be a good example.

The courts have recently adopted the view that it is not always enough to take reasonable steps to draw the other party's attention to the set of terms. If they contain an 'unusual' term, you must go further and do what is reasonably necessary to bring the *particular clause* that is unusual to the attention of the other party. This has long been the case with clauses attempting to exclude liability. What is an 'unusual' clause? The leading case concerned a clause permitting what one of the appeal judges called an 'extortionate' fee. One judge spoke of clauses that are 'particularly onerous', another of clauses that are not the 'usual terms regularly encountered' in that type of business. What steps might be taken to bring such an unusual clause to the attention of the other party? In another case Lord Denning suggested the use of red ink with a red hand pointing at the writing . . .

Life is much easier if you can do business with a document that embodies a *signed* written contract. We shall see later how a party is bound by an agreement he has signed whether or not he has understood it and whether or not he has even read it.

> *Troubleshooting. If your business uses its own standard terms, do they include an 'unusual' clause? Are you taking reasonable steps to bring it to the notice of customers/suppliers, or is it buried in a mass of small print?*

A set of clauses, headed 'Conditions' or 'Terms of Trading', may sometimes be found on the company's paperwork, such as an invoice, or perhaps in a separate leaflet. It could even be found in the brochure or price list. As we have already seen, to be valid the clauses must be introduced into the transaction before the agreement is concluded, ie before there is communication of an acceptance of an offer. If the terms appear on the back of an invoice sent to the customer, for example, the business has probably attempted to introduce them into the transaction too late.

A signed written contract

If the nature of the transaction permits, there are additional advantages in your business using a document that constitutes a signed written contract. This will incorporate the set of terms together with the other matters to be agreed for the individual deal, such as the price. If your business engages in different types of transaction, you will probably need more than one standard document, for example one for sales to consumers and one for sales to business. A signed written contract has two main advantages:

1. It underlines the importance of the transaction in most people's eyes and strengthens their commitment to the deal. Presumably this is due to the widespread misconception that unless what has been agreed is in writing it is not legally binding.

2. Appropriate written documentation helps to give the business the appearance of professionalism and efficiency. And the use of appropriate documentation *is* professional and efficient.

The nature of your business (eg whether your goods are standard lines described in sales literature or custom made) to a large degree dictates your business operations and method of working. The manner in which customers and suppliers interface (eg whether representatives are used who fill in the documentation) is also so varied that only those with knowledge of a business's operations can know which document could set out the terms of the agreement and provide for the other party's signature. If, for example, your work has to be individually priced, you will presumably have to notify the other party once you have ascertained it, and specify the work to be undertaken. It may be your practice to send a document setting these out; do you feel this could serve to record the terms of the agreement?

If you send such a document to a customer who then responds with an order by letter or telephone, referring to the quotation, then so far as the law of contract is concerned this would be an acceptance of the terms set out in the quotation. In practice however, in the event of a dispute arising, the other party's reaction may be, 'I didn't agree to all that small print you sent'. The law of contract may be on your side and a judge would probably find in your favour, but it is better to pre-empt this reaction.

Your quotation, or whatever it is called, could make provision for the customer to sign it, to certify that he is accepting the quotation and proceeding on the terms set out. This could take the form of a tear-off slip which is then returned to you, but the disadvantage is that the customer does not have a copy of his own signature. If two copies of the quotation are supplied the customer can be asked to sign and date both, so that he retains a copy as a visual reminder to him of his signed assent.

Where the sale of goods is concerned, perhaps at present you may supply an order form for the customer to complete the details of the goods after they have received sales literature. Such an order form could set out the business's terms and provide for the customer's signature.

The layout of documentation

If you are a supplier of goods or services to the general public, rather than to other businesses, certain aspects of your documentation will need greater attention. But whether you are dealing with consumers or business people, they are still customers and there is no good reason why that documentation should not be user-friendly. However, members of the public are less accustomed to paperwork and may be put off signing something that looks like a legal document. The language might be too complex for them to understand – assuming they read it!

The appearance of the documentation can be made less daunting by relegating some of the text to the back. The front page could make provision for the name and address of the customer, place of delivery, price, and details of goods or services to be supplied. This could be rounded off by the customer's signature beneath a request to supply the goods/services *'detailed on the terms set out overleaf'*. These words are of course an attempt to forestall a later claim that the customer was not aware of the terms. It may also help to ward off such a claim if the clause recites that the customer certifies he has read the terms.

Where you are devising standard documentation for use by you as the buyer, the problem arises that some of the transactions will be of a one-off nature. It may not be practical to devise all-embracing documentation which can be used, for example, for the installation of central heating in the factory. On the other hand a great proportion of the goods and services you buy will be on a regular basis, for example, the purchase of components to be used in the manufacturing process. For these regular transactions many companies draw up a document commonly described as a purchase order, setting out the terms upon which they will buy. In practice, suppliers are more likely to have their own standard terms and documentation, so if the buyer does too, the likelihood is greater that there will be a clash of documentation: the battle of the forms. Where this clash does occur, generally speaking the purchaser will be in a stronger position than the supplier, because he is the customer. But in some instances lack of competition may tip the balance of bargaining power in favour of the supplier.

Order information

The documentation should record information needed in the various stages of processing the order. Some or all of the following matters may need to be referred to:

1. Order number.
2. Provision for a receipt, eg for a deposit.
3. Information for the sales office, eg how the enquiry was raised.
4. Identity of representative acting on behalf of the business.
5. Matters to be completed by the finance office, eg commission rate for sales representative; credit check on customer.

6. Mode of payment.
7. VAT number (if registered).
8. Information required by the Business Names Act 1985 and the Companies Act 1985 (see pages 68 and 69).

How many copies of the document will be required?

Trade associations' contracts

Many trade associations make available one or more standard contract forms for their members to use when contracting with other members or with outsiders.

In some trades use of these forms is widespread and it becomes the practice for those who work regularly with the standard contracts to simply refer in a particular transaction to the standard industry contract and agree that that shall be the terms on which they proceed. This is an acceptable way of contracting, provided it is perfectly clear which *particular* contract applies.

Notice that here we have adopted the common practice (for people in industry) of referring to the printed standard form provided by the association as a contract, whereas of course it will not become a contract until the parties have made their agreement.

If your business is not at present using standard terms or a written contract, and it could, it may be that your relevant trade association has these available for the use of members. This might be a reason for joining the Association of Paper Clip Manufacturers and Importers, or whatever. The cost of membership fees for the first couple of years or so might work out at less than the cost of having your own standard documentation expertly drafted by lawyers, and the association's documentation will, presumably, be updated periodically.

Mistakes in the document

We cannot leave the subject of written contracts without considering what would be the position if the documentation contains a mistake.

A mistake made by the parties to a contract will fall into one of two distinct types:

- the mistake relates to the content of their agreement; or
- the written document does not record accurately what they did agree.

For example, in the first problem, Supplier believes he is selling, and

Buyer believes he is buying, Grade 3 widgets – whereas they are in fact, unknown to them, dealing in Grade 2 widgets. Note that both parties have made a mistake, although they are in agreement; they both believe they are making a contract for Grade 3 widgets.

Such a mistake can arise in either written or oral contracts. Whichever, the law where both parties make the same mistake is not entirely free from doubt. It can be argued that the courts will only declare the contract a nullity when they have no alternative other than to do so – where in fact there is nothing to make a contract about, for example because, unknown to the parties, the goods did not exist. If the mistake is less serious than this, the court may at least refuse to help enforce it where one of the parties will not go ahead.

Another example is where Supplier is selling one thing and Buyer believes he is buying something else. Supplier thinks Buyer is buying Grade 3 widgets, Buyer thinks Supplier is selling Grade 2. Where the parties are at cross-purposes the court calls in its friend, the reasonable bystander, and asks, 'What do you think the parties agreed?' The scope for such mistakes is lessened where the parties have a written contract: the parties can take the opportunity to spell out clearly in writing what it is that they are to receive and to supply.

A much more common possibility is that only one of the parties makes a mistake. It would undermine the sanctity of contract to allow a party to ride free of his obligations simply because he has made a mistake as to what he is getting under the agreement, so the courts are reluctant to intervene and will do so only if the other party knew of the mistake (or must have known of it).

The second type of mistake, and one which arises with a written contract, is where the document does not record accurately what the parties agreed, eg the parties agreed to supply and buy Grade 3 widgets, but the document mistakenly describes them as Grade 2. In practice it is likely that the mistake will favour one of the parties who may then be reluctant to agree that the document misrepresents the agreement. In these circumstances it falls to the other party to convince the court that his view of what the parties agreed is the correct one, even though it is not reflected in the document. If the court is satisfied that the document is incorrect, it may order it to be amended to reflect accurately what the parties did agree – not to do so would otherwise frustrate the intention of the parties. But convincing the court can be a big hurdle.

All of which underlines the need for care in the preparation, and scrutiny, of written agreements.

What does the contract mean?

It is useful for those involved in making contracts to know how the court interprets what the contract says.

Lawyers call the process *construction*. We have already seen that the basic approach of the court is to use the test: 'What would a reasonable person think the parties agreed?' We stress again that this may not produce the same answer as: 'What did the parties intend to agree?'

How does the court set about determining what a contract means?

1. It generally declines to look at the prior negotiations. This may seem surprising, but the reasoning is as follows. If the parties exchanged draft clauses, before the final clause emerged, which used expressions different from those in the final version, what is the point of discovering the meaning of those abandoned expressions? If, however, the same expressions were used in the final document, it would be dangerous to discover their meaning in earlier versions because by the time of the final agreement the surrounding circumstances may have changed.

2. The court is seeking to discover the meaning of the contract *at the time the agreement was made*. Therefore the court does not look, generally, at the behaviour of the parties in carrying out the contract to see what they thought it meant *after* they had made it.

3. In contracts of the same type (eg building contracts, shipping contracts) where standard words are commonly used, to give consistency the court will usually interpret those words in the same way.

4. The court may take into account the commercial background against which the contract was made. This may entail the court recognising that in the particular trade in which the contract was made certain words have a meaning of their own for members of the trade.

5. The court may take into account whether or not the parties made use of a lawyer to draft the documentation. For example, an expression has been used which, in law, has a meaning other than its popular meaning in everyday speech. Where the services of a legal expert were used, the court would be likely to interpret the word as having the lawyers' meaning. The outcome could also be affected where the contract has ousted some rule, eg the post rule that we looked at in Chapter 3, or some term that would otherwise be implied. Where the contract appears to contradict

such a rule or implied term, the court is more likely to take the view that it has been ousted where the documentation was drawn up by legal personnel, because they would have been aware of the rule or implied term and thus aware of the consequences of the contradictory provision in the written documentation. In other words, the lawyer would have known the effect of what he was doing!

Should you use a lawyer?

Some aspects of the courts' interpretation of written contracts afford good reason to draw up a set of standard terms or other contractual documentation only in conjunction with a 'legal eagle'.

For some small businesses, however, the likely costs of using the services of the lawyers will either deter the proprietors from the task of having their own terms/documentation, or tempt them into a DIY effort, perhaps by stealing the terms of a competitor in the same trade.

By using the services of a good solicitor you may save money. Expenditure now on a prudently drawn set of terms or documentation could one day save you many times that sum in legal fees in a dispute that could have been avoided – plus the saving in anxiety, and the time spent away from the business in meetings with lawyers preparing your case.

Chapter 5

Contents of the Contract – Preliminary Matters

Before we consider in detail the contents of your contract, there are certain preliminary matters to which you should give attention - matters that will become all-important if the contract is broken.

The boundaries of the contract

Prior to the finalising of an agreement, much may be said or written by the parties. How do you decide what is a part of the contract and what is not? If something said or written *is* a term of the contract and it is not complied with, that will be a breach of contract. However, it is not always easy to decide what is and what is not within the walls of the contract.

If the parties intended that their agreement should be entirely in writing, then presumably something spoken that is not to be found in the written document was not intended to be a term of the contract. With contracts that are partly oral and partly in writing, it can be particularly difficult to decide what was, and what was not, within the contract. In the run-up to concluding the agreement one of the parties, especially the supplier, may make statements intended to persuade the other to make the contract. Such a statement is called a *representation*. A representation, although very important from the buyer's point of view because that was one of the reasons why he made the deal, may nevertheless not become a part of the contract.

In the case of a false statement made to induce the other to enter into the contract, a *misrepresentation*, the innocent party is very far from being without a remedy. But the remedies are not identical to those for breach of contract, so where matters go wrong it is still necessary to decide whether the statement relied on amounted to a representation or a term of the contract. As we shall see on page 55, where a term of the contract is broken, the innocent party may still be bound by the contract and have to carry out his side of the deal. If a misrepresentation worked, and the other party was induced by it to enter into the contract, then they may be able to set the whole contract aside. Where such a *rescission* of the contract is possible, both parties are put back in their original position – for example the buyer gives back the goods and the seller gives back the money.

The reasoning behind allowing the innocent party to set the contract aside for misrepresentation is that a party should not be bound by a contract he would not otherwise have entered into. But the right to rescission can be lost in a number of ways, including where the wrongdoer himself believed the statement was true and it would be out of proportion to the harm done to set the contract aside, although the wrongdoer could still be liable to pay damages.

Because the remedy for misrepresentation can be so all-embracing it behoves the business and those through whom it acts to take especial care to ensure the accuracy of statements made with a view to inducing the other to enter into the contract.

The relative importance of contractual terms

Not everything that the parties agree will be of equal importance. For example, it may be of the utmost importance to the customer buying a secondhand van for his business that the vehicle is a one-owner specimen. It will not be so important that the salesperson has promised to fix a blow in the exhaust before the van is delivered.

The importance of a term will come to matter if and when that term is broken. If the term was of importance to the party who was relying on it, it may be that now it has been broken he no longer wants to continue with the deal. When a transaction is going wrong and the other party is not keeping to their side of the bargain, our reaction will typically be: 'Have I still got to go on with this deal?' In a contract for the sale of goods where the seller is in breach of what was agreed: 'Do I have to keep these goods? Do I still have to pay for them?' To a lawyer, the aggrieved party is asking: 'Am I still bound by the contract even though the other party has broken it?'

The law recognises that not all terms are of equal importance and therefore categorises them accordingly. Until comparatively recently it could be said that the law recognised two categories, but now a third has emerged, because judges feel that a simple split into two types does not always lead to a just conclusion in a dispute.

The three categories of terms of the contract are *warranties, conditions* and *intermediate stipulations*.

Warranties and conditions

The word warranty has a restricted meaning to a contract lawyer, which does not coincide with the use of the word by business people. In everyday speech warranty refers to a guarantee by a supplier to put right defects which appear in goods or services.

The word condition can also have a different meaning to a contract lawyer from that which is in everyday usage to denote an event to which something is subject. For example, you promise to lend a friend your car on condition that he will put petrol in it. Indeed, the word condition is particularly troublesome. When making a contract the word can be used both in the narrow legal sense to label a particular type of term *and* in its everyday sense, to denote an event to which something is subject; we will look at this use of the word in contract law later in this chapter. Unfortunately, it is also common practice for a business to label its set of standard terms 'Conditions', as in the description, 'Terms and Conditions of Business'.

The terms of the contract are traditionally divided into two categories, major terms and minor terms. Lawyers call the major terms of the contract conditions and the minor or, more accurately, subsidiary terms warranties.

When things go wrong it is most important to be able to identify to which category a particular term belongs. The rights of the parties in the event of a breach of contract depend on whether the term is a condition or a warranty. Where the term broken is a warranty, the innocent party may sue for compensation for the harm he has suffered in consequence, but he is still bound by the terms of the contract and must go on with his side of the deal. Where, for example, a buyer of goods finds on delivery that they are subject to a defect which amounts to a breach of warranty, the buyer must still take delivery of the goods and pay for them. He will, however, be entitled to compensation for harm caused by the breach. In practice, rather than opting to sue for compensation he may deduct what he is entitled to from any payment he is due to make for the goods – the lawyers call this a 'set-off'.

Where a failure by one party amounts to a breach of condition, the rights of the other party take on a new dimension. The aggrieved party is entitled to treat the contract as being at an end and himself freed from his further obligations under the agreement. However, while he is entitled to take this action, usually he can, if he so wishes, elect to go on with the contract. For example, if the buyer of a secondhand van discovers on delivery that it is not a one-owner vehicle, even though the parties intended this to be a condition of the contract, he may prefer to keep the vehicle. If he has not paid for it he could take an appropriate reduction in the payment price. This could suit him where, for example, it would be difficult to obtain an alternative elsewhere.

Where the transaction does go wrong, the position of the innocent party thus depends on the nature of the term which the other party has broken. If the innocent party wishes to be freed of his obligations and to put an end to the contract, he must ascertain whether or not the term broken amounted to a condition. If he misinterprets the status of that term this could have the direst consequences. Where the term broken amounts only to a warranty and the innocent party misinterprets it as a condition and refuses to go on with his side of the bargain he will himself be in breach of contract. Indeed, if the obligation he refuses to perform amounts to a condition, then he would have committed a breach of contract graver than that of the original wrongdoer.

Thus a party to a contract can, first, find himself facing a breach by the other party and, second, be on the receiving end of legal action for a breach of contract which he has erroneously committed and which would not have occurred if the original wrong-doer had carried out his side of the bargain. The innocent party may indeed feel aggrieved.

It is therefore most important to be able to identify whether a term of the contract amounts to a condition or a warranty.

Is the term a condition or a warranty?

The answer to this question depends on what the parties intended. However, ascertaining the relative importance attached to a term by the parties can be a difficult process. A useful test is to ask: 'Would the party relying on the clause have made the contract at all if it had not been there?' After all, if the innocent party would not have entered into the transaction without being promised *x*, now that he is not to receive *x*, surely he should be allowed to free himself from the transaction.

Thus whether or not a term amounts to a condition is a question of fact in all the circumstances. It might be thought that to avoid agonising over the status of a term in the event of a breach, the question could be resolved decisively by providing expressly that a particular term shall amount to a condition or a warranty as the case may be. In practice, however, with a standard form contract drafted in the interests of one side only, there is a temptation for the party whose terms they are, to be too willing to describe terms as conditions. This is in the belief that liberally describing the other party's obligations as conditions is giving the greatest protection to the party whose terms they are by allowing that party to ride free in the event of a breach of the obligation. It is sometimes intended as an incentive to the other side to make sure they do not commit *any* breaches. All too often, alas, the term is used without knowing its full meaning.

This temptation to describe as a condition a term which in reality amounts only to a warranty can backfire. The court or arbitrator may in the event declare that a term labelled condition did in fact only amount to a warranty, but the innocent party may have relied on the description in the contract to regard themselves as freed of their obligations. Now the court is saying that the clause is not as described.

At first sight this may seem surprising, the natural reaction being that it is for the parties to label the clause. The approach adopted by the courts is, however, justifiable; a piece of timber remains a piece of timber and is not transformed into a table merely because its proud owner has labelled it as such. Thus if in truth a term of the contract amounts only to a warranty it cannot be converted into a condition by misleadingly labelling it as such.

L Schuler AG v Wickman Machine Tool Sales Ltd (1973)

Schuler contracted to give Wickman the sole right to sell its presses in the UK. Clause 7 of the agreement provided that 'it shall be a condition of this agreement that Wickman shall send its representative to visit . . . at least once in every week' the six big UK motor manufacturers. Wickman breached the clause on a number of occasions. *The court held* that the term did not on its true construction amount to a condition. Thus Schuler were not entitled to treat Wickman's breach of the clause as a breach of condition, and Wickman were entitled to damages.

Intermediate stipulations

An example will convey why it is that the courts have come to the realisation that the simple division into major terms and subsidiary ones does not always lead to a just conclusion. Let us suppose that Wonder Widgets Ltd have received an initial order for their wonderful widgets from the United States. The American importers have agreed that on receipt of the widgets, subject to their being as described (which they are), they will take and pay for a second consignment. This amounts to the biggest order Wonder Widgets Ltd have ever received, but it is, however, dependent on the initial batch of widgets being received in New York on a specified date, in time for the importers to show the widgets at the forthcoming World Fair. To comply with this deadline Wonder Widgets Ltd will have to get this first consignment of widgets on board a ship leaving Southampton docks at 6 am tomorrow morning.

Wonder Widgets Ltd agree with Whizz Carriers Ltd that Whizz will pick up the consignment from Wonder Widgets' premises and transport it to Southampton in time for it to be loaded on to the ship for sailing at 6 am. Whizz Carriers Ltd undertake the assignment knowing the circumstances, and appreciating the urgency of the matter.

Due to their inefficiency, Whizz Carriers fail to deliver the consignment to Southampton docks until shortly after 6 am. However, due to poor weather conditions, the ship's sailing has been delayed; the consignment is loaded on to the ship, and it sails shortly afterwards. The ship makes up the lost time, the goods arrive in America, the massive American order goes through. No harm of any sort is suffered by Wonder Widgets Ltd.

If we apply the test that we looked at earlier to decide whether a term is a condition, the answer here would almost certainly be yes. Would Wonder Widgets have entered into the contract with Whizz Carriers unless they had been assured that the goods would be transported to Southampton docks in time for the ship's sailing at 6 am?

Whizz Carriers had good fortune on their side and, despite their failure to comply with their promise, Wonder Widgets have suffered no loss. It would seem unduly harsh then if Wonder Widgets were able to declare the contract at an end after Whizz Carriers failed to get the consignment on to the ship by 6 am. Would it be entirely just that Wonder Widgets Ltd were freed of their obligation to pay for the services they had received from Whizz Carriers?

It is in circumstances like these that the courts have felt it would accord more with justice if the law was to encourage a policy of 'wait and see'. The courts have recognised that with some terms the rights of the innocent party should depend upon the outcome of the breach. A term may be of such a nature that the possible consequences of its breach range from grievous loss to the innocent party at one end of the scale, to immaterial importance at the other end. In such a case the consequences will determine whether the innocent party is entitled to treat the breach as breach of a condition – freeing them of their obligations under the contract – or only breach of a warranty, in which case they are themselves still bound. A term of this nature is an intermediate stipulation.

How bad do the consequences have to be before the innocent party is entitled to treat the breach as a breach of condition? The following test seems to have emerged: as events have turned out, has the innocent party been deprived of the substantial benefit that they were to receive under the contract? If we apply that test to the example of Wonder Widgets, the answer would surely be no. Accordingly, Wonder Widgets Ltd will not have been freed of their obligations under the contract and will have been bound to pay for the services rendered.

The disadvantage of the concept of the intermediate stipulation – also known as the innominate term – is that it introduces a further element of uncertainty. Recent cases have recognised the need for certainty in commercial situations; that it is desirable for the parties to know exactly where they stand at the time of the breach of contract. The court's willingness to nourish this modern third category of term appears to have waned somewhat of late. The attraction of the old simple division into major and subsidiary terms has begun to shine brighter again.

A second use of the word 'condition'

We mentioned earlier that in addition to its primary use to denote a major term of the contract, contract lawyers also use the word condition in its everyday sense, to denote an event to which something is subject.

This secondary use of the word occurs where the parties wish to make an agreement but do not want to bind themselves unless and until a certain event occurs, eg one of the parties is able to arrange the finance.

It is useful for a contracting party to be aware of the options open to them in this situation. It may be that both parties wish to make the arrangement so that there is nothing binding on either side and both are free to withdraw entirely at their option before the event occurs, as in the practice of making agreements to buy land and buildings 'subject to contract'. The expression is shorthand for 'subject to the preparation and approval of a formal written contract'. The meaning is clear: either party is free to withdraw until the event to which their agreement is subject – the preparation and approval of a formal written contract – occurs.

In other circumstances the parties may not wish either side to be able to withdraw. They will be bound if the condition is fulfilled and free only if it is not.

Another possibility is that the parties wish to place an obligation on one of them to attempt to bring about the condition. This might occur where an agreement is subject to one of the parties raising the finance. Is that party to be under an obligation to at least attempt to raise the money?

Each of these variations – and others – on the extent to which the parties are bound, if at all, is possible. The agreement must be suitably worded to reflect what effect the parties intend the condition to have.

Compensation

The innocent party to a broken contract will be entitled to sue for compensation for harm he suffers, whether it was a breach of warranty or a breach of condition. A sum of money awarded by the court as compensation is termed *damages*, a term which non-lawyers not unnaturally find confusing because the compensation is being sought for the damage that has been done.

It is often assumed that the court will order the contract-breaker to carry out the contract. In fact the court will only do so in a small minority of cases; the usual remedy for breach is damages. The court will only order the contract to be performed – it issues a *decree of specific performance* – where a sum of money would not be a sufficient remedy. An example would be a contract to sell the Mona Lisa. The buyer could not take his compensation and go elsewhere to buy another one. But if the contract was to supply a Ford Escort, the buyer can easily purchase a comparable car from another supplier.

Liquidated damages clause

The object of damages is to put the innocent party, as near as possible, into the position he would have been in if the contract had been performed. Rather than suffer the expense and delays of going to court to have the amount of compensation decided by the judge, the parties may make provision in their contract for a specified sum to be awarded in the event of a breach. Such a clause is known as a liquidated damages clause. It is not always possible for the parties to estimate the compensation and so they cannot include such a clause, but sometimes it is quite feasible to arrive at a figure.

Where a liquidated damages clause is included, the sum specified will be what the innocent party receives, even if the estimate was wrong. The innocent party may therefore end up with a sum either less or more than his actual loss. Sometimes the sum provided for in the clause is not a genuine estimate of the likely losses. This can occur, for example, where there is not equality of bargaining power and one of the parties includes a clause in his standard terms providing for compensation which will give him a 'profit' over the amount he would lose in the event of non-performance by the other. The courts call this a penalty clause. Unfortunately, and confusingly, genuine liquidated damages clauses are often labelled 'penalty clause' by the parties to the contract. If the clause really is a penalty clause it will be void and unenforceable.

Arbitration

In the event of a dispute over the contract, the parties may prefer it to be determined by a third party, an arbitrator, rather than pursue the matter through the courts. The main advantages of arbitration are the absence of publicity and the opportunity to have the dispute adjudicated by someone who has specialised experience and knowledge relating to the matter. For example, in a dispute between the parties to a building contract the arbitrator can be a surveyor.

Other liability

We should point out that, in making a contract, liability to the other contracting party does not exhaust the possibilities for legal liability. The law of contract is one of two great fundamental branches of civil law. It is concerned with rights and obligations we assume voluntarily by entering into a contract. The law of *torts* relates to obligations imposed upon us by law whether we want them or not. It provides remedies for those to whom we cause harm by our actions. We all suffer harm in our day-to-day lives and it is neither possible nor desirable for the law to give us a remedy for every example. But during the past few decades the law has cast its net wider, and has held more people legally liable for their failure to do something. Yesterday no liability attached to harm caused by failing to do *xyz;* today you may be liable.

By the act of making a contract you are today putting yourself in an arena of potential liability to other people with whom you have *not* made the contract; for example, third parties who suffer loss due to your failure to carry out the contract properly. Thus in a recent case, a building society made a contract with a firm of surveyors to value a property on which the society proposed to grant a mortgage. The surveyor, in breach of his duty under the contract to use reasonable skill, failed to notice a defect in the property, which then had to be put right by the society's borrower. The borrower sued the surveyor and recovered his loss; the surveyor knew that his valuation would be communicated to the borrower and that he would probably rely on it in deciding whether to buy. If the surveyor had not entered into the contract with the building society he would not have found himself in a position of potential liability to this third party.

A further possibility of liability, not under the law of contract but under the law of torts, is to the other contracting party and arises in the following way. In the 1960s the courts, reversing the previous position, held that a person can be liable for statements he makes negligently to another which cause that other person financial loss. In one case a famous petrol company was negotiating to lease out one of its petrol stations to the plaintiff. A representative of the company gave the other party his opinion, based on his experience, of the likely throughput of petrol at the station. The plaintiff entered into the contract in reliance on the opinion, which was given without proper thought and proved to be over-optimistic. The company was held liable.

The law in this area of negligent statements is not yet fully settled. For now, it is at least clear that a negligent statement made by one party during the course of negotiations to the other *may* give rise to a claim for damages in the law of tort.

It is appropriate to warn here also that the giving of an opinion to the other contracting party prior to concluding the agreement could in certain circumstances amount to a misrepresentation. It will be recalled that a representation is a statement made with a view to inducing the other party to enter into the contract. This has to be a statement of *fact*, eg 'This car was previously owned by a little old man who only used it to go to church on Sundays'. However, by the act of venturing the opinion, the party making the statement could be conveying the impression that he knows facts which lead him to the opinion. If he doesn't know them, then this is in itself a misrepresentation.

Terms implied into your contract

We have seen earlier that both the courts and Parliament put into your contract terms which you have not expressly agreed with the other party. You will recall that in the case of a contract for the sale of goods you may, if you wish, leave it for the Sale of Goods Act to supply a set of terms and rules to govern the rights and duties of the parties, including such vital matters as time of payment, when delivery shall be, and when the goods shall become the buyer's property. We also saw that the parties may devise the contract themselves, making their own provisions rather than relying on the Act.

However, some of the terms implied by the Sale of Goods Act cannot be ousted by what you have expressly agreed; and quite possibly these terms are not to your liking. This occurs in consumer contracts. The main characteristic of a consumer contract is that it is one made with a person who does not buy in the course of a business. This method of implying terms into a contract is the law's main vehicle of consumer protection; this concept of the term which cannot be excluded applying to the millions of retail sales made with members of the public each day.

The principal terms implied by the Sale of Goods Act for the protection of consumers are found in sections 13 and 14 of the Act. (A hire purchase agreement is technically a contract of hire and not a contract of sale, but nevertheless terms almost identical to the following are also implied into a hire purchase contract.)

These all-important implied terms are:

- that where the goods have been sold by description, they will correspond with that description;
- that the goods be 'of merchantable quality';
- that where the buyer wants the goods for a particular purpose, they are fit for that particular purpose.

Troubleshooting. Is your business attempting unlawfully to exclude the statutory implied terms in consumer sales (by a notice, for example)?

These terms are in fact implied into *all* contracts made by a business for the sale of its goods, but in the case of a consumer contract they cannot be excluded. Indeed, to attempt to do so by, for example, an express clause purporting to exclude them, is an *offence* punishable by the criminal courts!

This fact appears to be not widely known in business and you can come across flagrant breaches of the law daily, usually by small businesses who do not have the benefit of a legal department and who have not yet been in dispute with their local consumer protection department. One of the easiest ways to fall foul of the law is to display a notice in retail premises to the effect that a refund of money cannot be made, perhaps because the goods are sale goods. Such a notice may amount to an attempt to exclude the terms implied in a consumer contract by sections 13 and 14 of the Sale of Goods Act. Of course, not all notices relating to refunds are unlawful; each case turns upon the wording of the notice. For example, the requirement as to merchantable quality does not apply where defects have been drawn to the attention of the buyer before sale, and a notice excluding refunds for such a defect would not be an attempt to exclude the general requirement as to merchantability.

Where the goods have been described

Where there has been 'a sale by description', the Sale of Goods Act implies a term into the contract that the goods supplied will correspond with the description of them made by the seller. When is a sale a sale by description? The courts seem to have changed their minds recently about what is meant by the expression. Certainly it will be a sale by description where the buyer has not seen the goods and is therefore doing the deal relying on a description. You probably buy goods without seeing them more often than you realise; if you pick up a packet of cornflakes from the supermarket shelf you will be relying on the description of the contents on the packaging. However, the fact that the buyer has seen the goods does not stop the sale being a sale by description; for example, the description may be of a characteristic which cannot itself be seen. So if a car described by the dealer as a 1990 turns out to comprise the front half of a 1989 welded to the back half of a 1991, there will be a breach of the implied term.

Until fairly recently it was thought that if anything was said or written about the goods which in some way identified them, this would make the contract a sale by description, and in some of the cases a very wide meaning has been given to description. However, it seems from recent comments by the higher courts that they are now less willing to label a contract a sale by description. This is partly because the implied term as to description, and the implied terms as to merchantability and fitness for a particular purpose, are made *conditions* by the Act. So under the Act a small deviation from the description of the goods entitles the buyer to consider himself freed from his obligations. It seems that in future the courts will be less inclined to label the sale a sale by description if the buyer has not *relied* on the description in making his decision to buy.

Description can include such matters as quantities, measurements, materials, method of packing, weight and ingredients.

Arcos Ltd v Ronaasen & Son (1933)

The sellers contracted to supply a quantity of staves described as being half an inch in length. When delivered the staves were too long by one-sixteenth of an inch. *The court held* that the sellers were in breach of the implied term as to compliance with the description, the buyers could reject the goods, and the sellers were liable in damages. One of the judges, Lord Atkin, said: 'a ton does not mean about a ton, or a yard about a yard. Still less, when you descend to minute measurements, does half an inch mean about half an inch.'

It is partly because of the effect of the implied term as to description that sellers will sometimes attempt to qualify statements as to size with words such as 'thereabouts' or 'approximately', thus allowing them a margin. Of course, where the buyer's requirements are for precise measurements, this may not be acceptable.

From the seller's point of view it is worth bearing in mind that the more detailed the description given of the goods, the greater the burden he places upon himself, because of the implied term that the goods must correspond with that description.

It should also be borne in mind that the *Trade Descriptions Act* makes it an offence punishable in the criminal courts to apply in the course of a business a false 'trade description' to goods. A 'trade description' only relates to a list of matters set out in the Act, although it is quite a long list, and includes size, performance, composition, history and method of manufacture. The Act is best known for its application to car dealers who supply cars with false mileages.

Merchantable quality

What is entailed by the requirement that goods should be of merchantable quality?

Broadly speaking, goods are of merchantable quality if they are fit for the purpose for which goods of that type are commonly bought. Shoes are commonly bought for the purpose of walking, so if the heel comes off when the buyer wears them for the first time the shoes clearly are not of merchantable quality. But the goods only have to be as fit for their common purpose as it is reasonable to expect in the circumstances. So, in deciding whether goods are merchantable, accounts must be taken of the price paid, how the goods were described, and whether or not they are secondhand.

Defects in the appearance of the goods, if serious enough, can make goods unmerchantable. In the case of a new car, for example, it has been said that the common purpose includes not merely driving it from *A* to *B*, but doing so with pride in its appearance. So if a new car develops rust on the bodywork it may be unmerchantable.

It may happen that a defect does not appear for some time – for how long must the goods be of merchantable quality? That is not an easy question to answer. Certainly, the goods must be of merchantable quality at the time of sale; therefore, if the buyer can show that the defect must have been present at that time, even though it has not manifested itself until later, then he will succeed in a claim based on merchantability. In one case, a towing hitch bought for a Land Rover broke due to its defective design, but not until 16 months after it was fitted. The court held that it was not of merchantable quality.

The fact that the defect is capable of being repaired does not prevent the goods being unmerchantable. It is not for the buyer to put matters right, since he is not getting what he has contracted for.

The terms and rules provided by the Sale of Goods Act to govern the rights of the parties can, as we have seen, be varied by express agreement; it is also possible for them to be negated by custom or usage of the trade. In one case, meat was sold to a retail butcher at Smithfield market, which proved to be unfit for human consumption. The buyer sued, claiming breach of the implied term that the meat was fit for its purpose. Evidence was brought that it was the prevailing custom at the market that there was no implied term that meat sold *was* fit for consumption, and that was therefore the basis on which the business had been transacted. The buyer lost.

Fitness for particular purpose

Where the buyer wants the goods for a particular purpose, a term is implied into the contract that the goods shall be fit for that particular purpose provided the buyer makes it known to the seller. This provision covers the situation where a buyer wants goods for a purpose which is not the ordinary purpose for which they are usually bought.

The term is highly relevant to exporters who are buying for sale to countries with regulations governing the product, such as safety regulations, or with particular climatic conditions.

The provision does not apply if it would not be reasonable for the buyer to rely on the seller's skill and judgement in the matter.

Buyer's remedies for breach of the section 13 and 14 terms

Each of these terms is given the elevated status of a condition by the Sale of Goods Act, and we have seen (page 55) that breach of a condition entitles the innocent party to treat the contract as being at an end. This means that the buyer can reject the goods and refuse to pay for them if any of these implied terms are broken; for example, the goods are not as described. This powerful option is, however, restricted by a further provision in the Act that, unless the contract provides otherwise, the right to reject the goods is lost once the buyer has accepted them.

Taken together, the three implied terms are wide-sweeping in their scope. They are used daily against sellers, not only by consumers but also by commercial buyers. A common response from the seller is the retort: 'But we didn't know about the defect.' Heard even more often is the cry: 'We've done our best – we can't do any more.' If the goods are not fit for their purpose, neither of these assertions is a defence. In effect, the seller is saying that he is not at fault, has not been negligent; but the obligation placed upon him by the implied terms as to merchantability and fitness for particular purpose is strict.

'I've done my best' may not be good enough for the law of contract.

Chapter 6

Contract for the Sale of Goods: The Basics

What are you going to put into your contract? What are the matters that you have to consider?

We shall examine first the contents of a contract for the sale of goods, since percentage-wise this is the most important type. A contract for the sale of goods can at times be of great complexity; we will start by looking at a straightforward sale of specific goods and this chapter will consider the basic matters to be agreed.

You will recall that should the parties so wish they may leave it to the Sale of Goods Act 1979 to provide the terms of their contract and the rules governing the obligations and rights of the parties. While considering the clauses that you might put in your contract, we shall refer to your position under the Act, if you do not make your own provision.

Both parties to a contract will wish to be informed on the following essentials:

- Who is making the contract?
- What is being sold?
- What is the price?
- When is payment to be made?
- When will the buyer receive the goods?

Who is making the contract?

This question may not always be as straightforward as it would appear.

Do the parties have the power to make the contract?

A good salesperson should ask himself long before the stage of closing the deal: 'Has the person I am negotiating with the authority to make the contract?' Generally speaking, if a business puts somebody in a position where it is reasonable for outsiders to believe that they have the authority to do what they are doing, then they shall be deemed to have that authority even though in fact they have acted beyond their powers. For example, the partnership agreement in a business may restrict the type of contract a partner can make on his own authority, but if he is making a contract of a type which outsiders would expect him to have authority to make, then the partnership will be bound by what he has done. Of course, this will not be so if the other contracting party *knew* that the partner did not have the authority, or if they ought to have known in the circumstances.

In the case of a registered company there is a further complication beyond whether or not its directors or employees have power to make that contract on the company's behalf – does the company itself have power to make the contract? Unlike an ordinary person, a company cannot simply make any contract. It can only do what is authorised by its constitution, to be found in the documents submitted when it was registered. In one case, a company which was set up and authorised by its constitution to carry on the business of an introduction agency then went into pig farming. The contracts made in its pig farming business were held to be void. In practice, this question of company powers is not now the problem that it was in the past. On Britain's entry into the European Community, the law was changed to bring us into line with the other member states. Broadly, the present position is that a person dealing with a company in good faith will not be bound by restrictions on the powers of the company of which they were unaware.

But should you suspect that the company is not authorised to do what it proposes, and you then close your eyes and don't check the position, you are in danger. Remember, you must be acting in good faith to clothe the contract with validity. In order to find out the powers of the company and its officers you can ask to see the company's memorandum and articles of association. If you don't want it to look as if you are impugning integrity, you can inspect them at Companies House.

Using a business name

Many people involved in business are not trading under their own name. John Smith, for example, may trade as Grease Garage, but you cannot make a contract with Grease Garage. A person or a company has the power to make a contract, and Grease Garage is neither. It is simply the trading name of John Smith. So the contract will have to be made by John Smith.

If you are about to make a contract with 'Grease Garage' how can you find out whose name should be on the contract? As John Smith is using a trading name, he must comply with the Business Names Act 1985.

Unfortunately, John Smith almost certainly has never heard of that Act. In the experience of the authors the Act is little known among business people and its provisions are widely flouted by small businesses. The Business Names Act provides that where a business is being carried on in a name which is not that of the proprietor (or the partners) then these names must be stated on certain documentation, including letter headings, orders for goods, and invoices. It is from these that you will know who you are dealing with. If your business uses a trading name you will, no doubt, be complying with the Act. Remember that a contract might be embodied in documentation which has to comply with the provisions of the Act, eg a purchase order. Failure to observe the provisions of the Act amounts to a punishable offence, and if the business brings proceedings to enforce a contract made where it has breached the Act's provisions, in certain circumstances the court may refuse to allow the business to pursue its claim under the contract.

The Act also applies to registered companies. When a company is formed, just as when a person is born, it will be given a name, though in this instance the name will be that given in the register of companies. Very often a registered company does not use its registered name in its business operations, for example, because the name is commercially unattractive. A company which is trading under a name other than its registered name must also disclose that registered name on the documentation we mentioned.

A company also has to comply with the Companies Act 1985, which requires additional information to be given on order forms and letterheads. This includes its company registration number and the address of its registered office.

> *Troubleshooting. Is your business complying with the Business Names Act 1985? Does your letterheading disclose to potential contracting parties who they are dealing with? Do your purchase order forms contain the details required by law?*

What is being sold?

It makes sense for the parties to the contract to spell out what is being sold, in order to avoid disputes about what is being received and to avoid disappointing the business's customers. If your customers are the general public rather than business people it is probably fair to assume that many of them will act in a less than businesslike manner. They will not be as clear in their own minds as they should be about what they are to receive.

This need for clarity is more important when there are alternative specifications or options available. Rather than leave a blank space on the documentation for completion it is more prudent to set out those alternatives or options on the documentation and ask the person completing it to indicate those which apply, perhaps by deleting any that are not required. This procedure will lessen the possibility that some detail or other will be omitted.

Sales literature, such as a catalogue or a leaflet, will probably contain statements describing the goods in some way. Has the specification of the goods changed since the sales literature was prepared? It is possible to put a disclaimer in sales literature pointing out that specifications, prices etc change and that the current situation should be checked by the buyer.

What is the price?

It would be unusual for a buyer and seller to agree the sale of goods without mentioning the price. Instead of fixing the price in the contract they may, however, want to provide some mechanism for determining how the price shall be arrived at, for example, by the expert valuation of a third party.

If the parties do not specify the price payable under the contract, the Sale of Goods Act provides the answer: the price shall be a 'reasonable' price. What is reasonable is of course a question of fact to be determined in all the circumstances. Omitting to agree the price and relying instead on this provision is obviously not to be recommended.

The last few decades, with their periodic bursts of high inflation, have witnessed the increasing use of clauses which allow the price to be varied by the seller. The clause often provides that the price prevailing shall not be the price current at the time the agreement is made, but the price ruling at the time the goods are delivered to the buyer. There may be a considerable interval between the making of the agreement and the date of delivery, for example where the goods are being made to the buyer's specifiction. In these circumstances a price variation clause is more likely to be found in documentation drafted by the suppliers – and likely to be resisted by the buyers when they read the supplier's terms.

When is payment to be made?

It is unlikely that the seller will fail to indicate when payment is to be made. If, however, there is no understanding between the parties on the point, the Sale of Goods Act provides that the buyer must be ready to make payment when the goods are delivered.

This is a timely point at which to give a reminder that if the sale is to a consumer and the business is granting credit to the customer, the agreement will be governed by the Consumer Credit Act. The Act requires the agreement to be in writing and makes detailed provision as to its contents and the manner in which the document is laid out. Even the size of the print is governed by law in such a contract.

The time of making payment is only one of the factors to be considered. Others include:

- How is payment to be made?
- Is a deposit payable?
- Is there to be a discount, for example for payment with order?

How is payment to be made?

Where payment is made by cheque, the seller may wish to retain ownership of the goods until the cheque has been cleared.

Many business people endeavour in this situation to retain possession of the goods and erroneously believe that while they retain possession they retain the ownership of them. A moment's reflection reminds us that possession and ownership are not the same thing: x may be legally in possession of y's goods, although y is the owner, because, for example, y has lent them to x. Many people are surprised to learn that in a contract for the sale of specific goods, the basic proposition is that the ownership of the goods passes to the buyer *when the agreement is made*, unless the parties make it clear that this is not their intention. (We will be returning to this very important consideration in Chapter 7.) However, the buyer is not entitled to delivery of the goods unless and until he is able and willing to pay for them. Nevertheless because ownership of the goods has passed when the agreement was made, this enables the buyer to resell the goods and pass on the ownership that has passed to him under the contract. In practice, of course, this could be difficult where the buyer did not yet have possession of the goods.

When will the buyer receive the goods?

First, whose job is it to deliver the goods? Should the seller transport the goods or the buyer collect them from the seller's premises? If the terms of the agreement remain silent, then the Sale of Goods Act provides (where we are dealing with a straightforward sale of specific goods) that the seller's premises will be the place of delivery; in other words, the buyer will collect them from the seller. If the goods are not at the seller's premises and the parties knew this when the agreement was made, then that location will be the place of delivery: the buyer will collect the goods from that place.

Other considerations in relation to delivery include:

- Is the date for delivery fixed or estimated?
- Is notice to be given when the goods are ready for delivery?
- Can there be a change in delivery date?
- What happens if the goods are late?

If no provision is made in the agreement for a delivery date, the Sale of Goods Act provides that delivery should be made within a reasonable time. What is a reasonable time is a question of fact to be determined in all the circumstances.

In a contract where both the buyer and the seller are in business, if delivery is late the courts have tended to the view that delivery is 'of the essence of the contract' and that late delivery effectively amounts to a breach of condition. Thus the buyer would be entitled to treat the contract as being at an end and himself freed from his obligations, including the obligation to take delivery of the goods. Clearly, it is hard on the seller if the buyer rejects the goods for late delivery: not only will he lose the profit on the transaction, but also the cost of carriage. The seller may therefore choose to spell out in his terms that time of delivery is *not* of the essence of the contract, meaning that the buyer does not have the right to reject the goods for late delivery, although the seller would still be liable to pay damages where the buyer suffers harm due to breach of this obligation. The seller may also try to transact business on the basis that delivery dates are not fixed but are estimates only of the likely date. He would then be able to argue that he is not in breach of contract if delivery is made within a reasonable time of the estimated date.

What happens when, as is not uncommon, the seller delivers the wrong quantity? The Sale of Goods Act provides that unless otherwise agreed the buyer can reject the goods, thus treating the contract as being at an end. However, if he accepts the quantity delivered he must pay for them at the contract rate.

The seller may have good reasons to make an express provision enabling him to deliver less than the agreed rate: for example, his own supplies may be erratic. For the seller, the problem is that such a clause may come within the provisions of the Unfair Contract

Terms Act 1977. We shall look at this important Act in some detail in Chapter 7; it arises here because it governs, among other contractual matters, attempts to allow one party to perform less than was expected under the contract. Whether or not such a clause is valid depends upon the Act. For now, it can be said that if the seller is not confident that he will be able to supply the quantity specified, it is better to provide in the contract for that situation than simply to leave the matter to chance. Such a clause *may* be valid under the provisions of the Unfair Contract Terms Act, and even if the court concluded that it was not valid, its inclusion may have had a deterrent effect upon the buyer, who might accept it at its face value and shrink from litigating on its validity.

Case study

The sets of clauses and documentation met in the fictional case study below (mentioned in the Preface) are not in any sense model contracts and each is defective or falls short in some way.

Alamo Carpet Warehouse is a retail carpet business located in a secondary high street in a Midlands city.

The business has recently been acquired by Alan Taylor who has given up his senior marketing post with a national chain of furniture warehouses. Alan has left his lucrative job with a big company to run his own smaller – for now – ship. Although he felt that his ex-company's marketing strategy of 'pile 'em high, sell 'em cheap' was becoming outmoded in the 1990s, nevertheless it was a very professional retail operation.

Alamo Carpet Warehouse is not quite such a professional operation. Set up by three partners in the late 1970s, for the last couple of years the Alamo ship has been steered through choppy waters by the remaining partner, Sid Green, a former replacement window salesman, now in his late fifties.

Alan has been doing some reading up in the last few weeks preparatory to his taking over and running his own business. His existing strengths lie in the field of sales and marketing, and he has bought two books on subjects in which he feels particularly weak: one was on finance and the other was *Making Contracts*.

Alamo occupies spacious but lightly heated premises, formerly a cinema. Alan stood outside his former cinema looking up at the fascia board announcing to the world the name of his new business: 'Alamo Carpet Warehouse'. He lowered his gaze to take in a view of the entrance. It was Monday morning and Day One of his first week as His Own Boss. As he stood facing the doorway that led into his empire, what he had done was beginning to sink in.

As a warehouse, there was no window display to entice shoppers in; instead a large sign on the wall depicted a hand with index finger pointing towards the entrance. Beneath the hand, Alan read: 'We shoot down the opposition with our prices'.

Sid Green was supposed to meet him at Alamo half an hour before opening time. Sid had agreed to 'come in' for the first week after the change of ownership to 'show him the ropes'. Alan, who had never had any direct involvement with selling carpet – no more than he had of running his own business – had asked Sid if he could be around for the first month or so, but Sid was going to the Bahamas on Friday morning.

Alan looked at his watch. Where was Sid? It struck him that Sid had never shown him how to operate the burglar alarm system.

From inside the premises there came a ringing sound. Alan put an ear up against the door: it was the phone. The salesman in Alan reacted – it might be a customer – it might be an order!

Alan spent an excited few minutes searching for the burglar alarm control against the background of the ringing telephone. The phone stopped ringing just before Sid arrived and told Alan that there was no burglar alarm.

Alan looked down the lines of roll upon roll of carpet and wondered whether the insurance company was happy that there was no alarm in premises with all this stock; the stock valuation of some of the better quality stuff had added up to far more than Alan had ever expected.

Sid was followed in by a postman who threw a solitary item of mail on to the desk, a brown window envelope.

Sid picked up the envelope. 'Here's your first letter as proud owner of Alamo Carpets,' he said to Alan. He opened the envelope, took out an invoice and looked at it. He grimaced. 'What a nerve! Look at that!'

Sid handed over the letter. Alan looked at it, but the figures meant nothing to him.

'That's for the roll out there that I've just moved,' said Sid. 'They've bunged the price up 80p a yard. And do you know who that's for? You remember that awkward woman who was in here start of last week when you was here?'

Alan tried to cast his mind back.

'You remember, that woman who talked really loud that I got you to deal with.'

Alan remembered.

'It took you nearly all the afternoon. And to top it all she was the one was adamant she weren't going to pay more than £5 a yard and you got me to let her have that – I told you it was a £5.99 line. Now they've gone and put it up to £4.80. It weren't worth doing the deal.'

Sid was clearly agitated. No wonder, Alan thought to himself, if his main supplier puts up prices after he has already quoted a price. Let's hope it doesn't happen too often, he thought.

Sid turned to go. 'I wouldn't mind, but it's always happening,' he said as he left.

Alan sat down in the boss's chair with a thoughtful expression on his face.

Manufacturing Ltd are Alamo's largest supplier. Alan had already notified them and other suppliers that he was taking over from today, although he hadn't yet heard anything from Manufacturing Ltd in response.

Alan told Sid that he hoped to make a profit on sales that he made and how was he supposed to do that if he didn't know what the line would cost him because their main supplier put up prices willy-nilly and charged whatever he felt like? Sid said they had always done it; he had just assumed that they could. Alan wanted to know what agreement he had with them, 'When we want something we ring them up and they send it,' was Sid's reply. No, he had never had any contract or anything like that – or not that he could remember.

It took them a long time to find the original correspondence dating back from when the account was opened. Within the file Sid was surprised to find a letter from Manufacturing Ltd confirming that an account had been opened and enclosing a copy of the company's terms of supply. Alan looked at the document, printed in blue ink on yellow flimsy paper. It wasn't the easiest and most inviting document to read.

'This reminds me,' said Sid. 'We'll have to ring through that order we took on Friday night just before we shut. If you don't ring it through before 12 noon we won't get it in time for Thursday and I've promised the woman.'

While Sid cleared drawers in his desk, Alan looked at the document and pondered. If he rang through and ordered now, would it be on these terms?

He was going to operate his new business in a professional manner. He decided he would read the document before ringing

Manufacturing Ltd's order department. He looked again at the printed document which had '1979' in the top right hand corner. He scribbled a note to remind himself when he did ring them to check that these terms were still current.

The document read as follows:

TERMS OF BUSINESS

1. Price
The price shall be the price set out in the company's price list current at the date the order is accepted by the company excepting that the price shall be adjusted to reflect increases in the price of raw materials prior to the date of delivery.

2. Payment
Payment must be made within 28 days of invoice date. Overdue accounts shall be charged interest at the rate of 2.5 per cent per month accruing daily.

3. Passing of Title
No title to the goods shall vest in the buyer until such time as payment in full of the sum due under the agreement has been made.

4. Guarantee
The goods supplied are guaranteed for a period of two years against defects in workmanship and materials. In any claims arising under this provision the goods shall be returned to the company carriage paid. The company shall repair or replace the goods at its discretion.

5. Alterations to the Order
No alterations to the order may be made by the buyer after confirmation of acceptance of the order has been sent by the company to the buyer.

6. Dye Matching
The company can undertake that dyes will match on two or more lengths of carpet in the same colourway only where these are ordered at the same time. No undertaking is given that dyes will match on items under subsequent orders.

7. Carriage Charges
All prices are ex-works and carriage shall be charged to the buyer at cost.

8. *Mis-delivery or Damaged Goods*

All claims for mis-delivery or damaged goods must be made within seven days.

At that point Alan came to a halt. Someone had spilled tea or coffee over the document and the rest of the terms were illegible . . .

Chapter 7

Contract for the Sale of Goods: Protecting the Seller

The terms of business sent out by Manufacturing Ltd in our case study at the end of Chapter 6 is an example of standard form documentation drafted by a supplier. The clauses are fairly typical of those we can expect to find in a standard form contract drawn up with the interests of the seller primarily in mind.

Some of the clauses in the document from Manufacturing Ltd touch upon the basics that we looked at in the preceding chapter, such as price. Other clauses have been inserted specifically to protect the interests of the supplier in the event of certain contingencies.

Let us look at some of the more important clauses in turn, to see why the supplier has included them and what their effect might be.

1. Price

The price shall be the price set out in the company's price list current at the date the order is accepted by the company excepting that the price shall be adjusted to reflect increases in the price of raw materials prior to the date of delivery.

The company has opted for an alternative to the price variation clause which we looked at in our review of basics in Chapter 6. That clause, it will be recalled, allowed the seller to charge the price stipulated in their price list at the time of delivery. Although no doubt the buyer will prefer the price to be fixed, that prevailing at the time the agreement is made, we saw that it is not uncommon for the supplier to attempt to recover a higher price. Manufacturing Ltd has opted for a halfway measure by attempting to recover a price increase that it has suffered before delivery, rather than charging the price set in its price list on the date of delivery, which might, of course, be much higher than the price ruling at the time the agreement was made. This new price could reflect market conditions which have occurred after the date of the agreement and enable the supplier to increase profit margins. Many buyers will live with the alternative clause provided here. They appreciate that if the suppliers have to bear price increases charged to them, they may end up with no margin for themselves. Other buyers will insist upon a fixed price.

2. *Payment*

Payment must be made within 28 days of invoice date. Overdue accounts shall be charged interest at the rate of 2.5 per cent per month accruing daily.

Alamo are benefiting from the common 28 days' credit provision. Manufacturing Ltd have prudently inserted a provision for interest to be payable on late accounts. It is a fact of life that many companies are slow payers, especially during periods of economic depression. There is no general provision in our law entitling creditors to interest for late payment, so without a clause like this the buyer is not entitled to interest on overdue accounts.

In practice, many buyers make late payment of the account without the interest due, but not so late that the suppliers consider it worthwhile chasing up what may be a comparatively small sum. Nevertheless, such a clause may have a deterrent effect on some buyers, and should certainly be considered by the sellers where the sum due under the credit arrangement is not trivial. If the sellers themselves have borrowed from the bank, their understandable attitude will be: we are paying interest – if debtors paid up on time we could reduce the interest *we* pay. Late payment also has a less obvious impact. Under inflation the sums due are devaluing in real terms. Three months' late payment during times of 10 per cent p.a. inflation is equivalent to about 2.5 per cent discount.

A further clause dealing with late payment is one which allows the seller to: (1) terminate the contract; (2) refuse to make further deliveries under that or any other contract the parties may have made. You might think that late payment by a buyer amounts to a breach of condition (a major term of the contract) which entitles the seller to regard the contract as at an end. The Sale of Goods Act provides, however, that in the case of late payment this is not so unless the contract provides otherwise. You might also think that if payment is not made by a seller, other supplies which have been contracted for can be withheld. Again, this is not necessarily so. Under the Sale of Goods Act, an unpaid seller has the right to retain possession of the goods and, where he has made part delivery, can retain possession of the remainder. However, this does not apply to a *severable contract*, where delivery is by instalments which are to be paid for separately. Default on payment of one instalment does not necessarily allow the seller to hold on to possession of the goods due under the next. This may come as a surprise to those who make such arrangements. Furthermore, if supplies are due under another contract already made with the same buyer, refusal to deliver could be a breach of that contract.

3.   *Passing of Title*
No title to the goods shall vest in the buyer until such time as payment in full of the sum due under the agreement has been made.

Use of the word 'title' indicates that the terms were probably drafted by a lawyer, either within the company's in-house legal department if it is big enough to have one, or by an outside firm of solicitors (who, in their turn, may have used the services of a barrister to carry out the drafting). The word that the lay person would use instead of title is probably ownership.

We saw in our review of the basics that under the Sale of Goods Act, unless a contrary intention is shown by the parties, in a contract for the sale of specific goods the basic proposition is that ownership in the goods will pass when the agreement is made; and that this entitles the buyer to sell on the goods before he has paid for them. Where the goods are not in a deliverable state (for example, in one case an engine was sold that was bolted to the floor of a factory), ownership does not pass until they are ready and the buyer has been notified.

Specific goods means those which have been identified and agreed upon at the time the contract is made: eg 'the Whizz 2000 photocopier in the showroom'. Often, of course, although the parties agree what the buyer is to receive, they do not identify the *actual* goods that will be delivered to him – what the Sale of Goods Act refers to as 'unascertained' goods. Alamo Carpets ordering carpet from their suppliers, the makers, is a good example of this. Alamo places an order with the makers for 40 metres of Springtime design in lilac colourway. They accept the order and send Alamo notification. Under the ordinary rules of contract that is a binding agreement for the supply of carpet as ordered, there having been an offer and a communicated acceptance. At the time the contract is made the specific carpet that Alamo will receive has not been identified. It is only when the order is processed and a piece of carpet of the required size is cut from the roll at the factory in accordance with the order, that the actual goods Alamo will receive under the contract will be identified. It can be seen that the ownership of those goods could not pass to Alamo until their identity was known. Once the goods have been identified and ear-marked to the contract, under the Sale of Goods Act the ownership of them will pass to the buyer unless the parties have agreed otherwise.

The object of clause 3 in Manufacturing Ltd's terms of business is to avoid ownership passing to the buyer before payment is made. It is known as a 'Romalpa' clause after the name of the leading case on the subject. The contract here is for the sale of unascertained goods. The clause can also be found in a contract for the sale of specific goods where, as we have seen, ownership would pass even earlier, when the contract was made.

The principal objective of a Romalpa clause is to deal with the situation where the buyer is in big trouble: the company is insolvent and is being wound up, or the bank or some other creditor has brought in the receiver. If ownership of the goods has been allowed to pass under the contract, the goods can be sold to pay off other creditors. The seller could then find that the secured creditors are paid out of the proceeds of the sale of the goods he supplied, while he remains unpaid.

A problem which can arise with such a clause is that in practice the buyer may need to re-sell the goods before he pays the seller's invoice; very often, the buyer will pay for the goods from the proceeds of his own re-sale. A clause can be put together by an expert draftsman under which the buyer is authorised to sell the goods, although they remain the property of the original seller, and the buyer must account to him for the proceeds of the re-sale.

4. Guarantee
The goods supplied are guaranteed for a period of two years against defects in workmanship and materials. In any claims arising under this provision the goods shall be returned to the company carriage paid. The company shall repair or replace the goods at its discretion.

A guarantee can be a valuable sales aid to a supplier, especially where the buyers are members of the public; although, ironically, consumers have greater protection than trade buyers. A guarantee is particularly attractive to the buyer where the product is technically complex or is new to the market. Although there may be good marketing reasons why a supplier wishes to offer a guarantee with his product, the offer is hedged round with legal restrictions.

The supplier's terms sometimes provide that the guarantee shall be in lieu of the implied terms of merchantability, fitness for purpose, and description, as implied by the Sale of Goods Act (see Chapter 5). The rights offered by the guarantee are probably not as extensive as those afforded by the implied terms and the seller is, in this way, attempting to cut down his potential liability. Protection of the consumer buyer is greater than that of the trade buyer because in a sale to a consumer these terms *cannot* be excluded; but in a commercial transaction between two parties in business the seller can attempt to exclude these implied terms. However, in practice such a clause will still be subject to the provisions of the Unfair Contract Terms Act. It will be recalled that the Act controls attempts to exclude or limit legal liability, commonly referred to as exclusion clauses. A clause in a commercial contract which attempts to exclude the implied terms is subject to the Act if, as is likely, it is contained in a standard form contract. Under the Act, an exclusion clause in a standard form contract is valid only to the extent that it is fair and reasonable.

The law has taken the view that it needs to intervene in standard form contracts because one of the parties is imposing such a clause on the other contracting party without regard to the individual circumstances of the deal. Where the parties individually negotiate a particular transaction and agree specifically that they will exclude or limit the liability of one of the parties in relation to that particular contract, the clause does not have to satisfy the criterion of being fair and reasonable. It is for the parties to negotiate and make their own deal.

George Mitchell (Chesterhall) Ltd v Finney Lock Seeds Ltd (1982)

The defendants, a firm of seed merchants, sold the plaintiffs 30 lb of winter cabbage seed, with which the plaintiffs planted some 60 acres. In error the defendants supplied autumn seed and the crop was a failure. A clause in the defendants' standard terms of sale limited their liability either to refunding the price or replacing the seeds. The plaintiffs sued for the value of the lost crop.

The court held that the clause was unreasonable. A factor to be taken into account was that insurance against a mishap such as delivering the wrong seed had been available to the sellers at a cost which, spread across their transactions, worked out at a very small sum per sale.

This requirement, that a clause purporting to exclude or limit liability must be fair and reasonable, does not apply solely to attempts to exclude the implied terms of merchantability, fitness for purpose and description. Any clause in standard form documentation which attempts to limit or exclude the legal liability of one of the parties to the contract is caught by this provision. Indeed, the Unfair Contract Terms Act spreads its net even further: *any* attempt to exclude or limit contractual liability, whether it is contained in standard form documentation or not, must be fair and reasonable *if it is in a consumer contract*.

Thus, a clause is subject to the fair and reasonable requirement if:

- it is contained in a contract with a consumer; or
- it is contained in a standard form contract.

So if your business deals with consumers, a clause which attempts to limit or exclude liability will be subject to the Act. If your business deals with trade customers, that clause will be subject to the Act unless it is part of a contract individually negotiated with the other side and not one entered into on standard terms which include such a clause.

In deciding whether, in all the circumstances, it is fair and reasonable to include the exclusion clause, the court will take into account the following factors:

1.   The relative bargaining strength of the parties.
2.   Whether the supplier's prices were cheaper because he had an exclusion clause.
3.   Whether the customer could have gone elsewhere to a supplier who did not impose an exclusion clause.
4.   Whether the other party knew of the existence of the clause and whether he knew of its extent.

Factor 3 is relevant because in some trades nearly, if not all, suppliers have an exclusion clause. This arises because the suppliers use terms of trading or a standard form recommended or supplied by their trade association. The customer will have no choice but to go to a supplier who will not accept full legal liability under the contract.

Factor 4 is aimed at the practice of burying exclusion clauses within a mass of other clauses, or using very small print, or coloured paper so that the printing is fainter than it would be on white paper. It will encourage lawyers who draft exclusion clauses to make them intelligible to the lay person.

Of course, if the clause is legible and noticeable the buyer may read it and decide he does not like it. He may then raise the matter with the seller, or he may simply not place an order.

The Unfair Contract Terms Act sweeps through contracts with a broad brush. It gathers up all kinds of terms that the lay person might pass over. So a clause is subject to the Act if it makes liability subject to conditions, or restricts the remedies open to the other party. For example, a commonplace clause providing that 'claims must be notified within 7 days', would be subject to the Act's scrutiny, as would a clause stating that defective goods must be returned to the seller carriage paid.

One point about exclusion clauses which would be of particular relevance to Manufacturing Ltd concerns a manufacturer's liability for unsafe products. Under the Consumer Protection Act 1987 (passed in consequence of the UK's membership of the European Community), a manufacturer (or importer) is liable for unsafe products that cause harm to consumers, even though he has not been negligent. The consumer who suffers harm – not just personal injury, this could be damage to his property – can sue the manufacturer without having to prove that the manufacturer failed to take reasonable care. No exclusion clause can exclude or limit this liability.

There is so much complex law surrounding exclusion clauses, some of which imposes criminal penalties, that any business which attempts to make use of a clause limiting or excluding liability should ask whether the clause has been subjected to the scrutiny of a (knowledge-able) solicitor. If the clause is in a set of terms or documentation supplied by a reputable trade association, one which keeps its documentation under review, then almost certainly you can relax. Otherwise, you should ask yourself whether the clause (or notice?) was originally drafted by a lawyer, or did someone in the firm copy a set of standard terms that was used by a previous employer or another firm in the same trade? Such corner-cutting measures are not unknown. Exclusion clauses are a minefield. If the clause is in documentation that was drafted by a lawyer, has it been reviewed since the Unfair Contract Terms Act was passed?

If there is doubt about any of this, and your organisation – or you – hesitates to pay a solicitor to advise on your documentation, look again at the Finney Lock Seeds case. The seller's revenue from the sale was £201.60 – minus damages paid of £61,513 and minus legal costs of hearings before the High Court, the Court of Appeal, the House of Lords, including the buyer's legal costs and services of Queen's Counsel.

If Alamo attempt to offer their own customers who are consumers a guarantee, as we have seen they cannot exclude the terms implied by the Sale of Goods Act. In addition they must make it clear that the guarantee is *not* attempting to do this. This is why the wrapping on your bar of chocolate undertakes to refund your money if you are dissatisfied, then states: 'The statutory rights of the consumer are not affected'. Failure to include a statement to this effect in close proximity to a statement relating to the rights of the consumer buyer amounts to a punishable offence under the Consumer Transactions Restrictions Statements Order, made by the Secretary of State for Trade and Industry.

Troubleshooting. If you supply a guarantee to consumers, does it refer to their statutory rights?

5. Alterations to the Order
No alterations to the order may be made by the buyer after confirmation of acceptance of the order has been sent by the company to the buyer.

Once the agreement has been made the seller is bound to supply and the buyer is bound to take the goods specified, but in practice buyers, especially where they are members of the public, are often under the delusion that they can unilaterally change their minds. A change to the order is of course an example of a variation of the contract (see Chapter 4).

Changes to the order are likely to incur inconvenience and expense to the seller who may feel he can do without this unnecessary complication. It is not uncommon to find a clause which, while not strictly necessary because it recites the existing legal position, is included as a deterrent to discourage inconvenient attempts to change the order.

Total refusal to consider alterations fails to recognise, however, circumstances in which the buyer has good cause to request them. This is particularly so where a trade buyer is selling on to his own customer and it is that customer who has requested the alteration; it may not be so easy for the buyer to adopt a non-cooperative attitude to his own customer. In practice it may be fairer to allow amendments up to the point at which the seller does not incur any disproportionate expense, but not beyond that stage. In Manufacturing Ltd's case it might have been more reasonable to include a clause accepting alterations to the order until the carpet had been cut from the roll. The clause need not be expressed as an *obligation* on the sellers to comply with a request for amendments, but can be couched in terms that they will undertake to make reasonable efforts up until the point indicated.

6. Dye Matching
The company can undertake that dyes will match on two or more lengths of carpet in the same colourway only where these are ordered at the same time. No undertaking is given that dyes will match on items under subsequent orders.

The seller is using his knowledge of the product to forestall problems that could arise in future transactions with the same purchaser. Carpet, like many other products, is subject to dye variations in different batches. One would expect trade customers to be aware of this, and the clause may be more necessary where customers are members of the public, who may not have given the matter any thought.

This clause is an example of how the product specification can lessen the likelihood of problems arising. When such documentation is being drawn, you could consult members of staff who have contact with customers; you could draw on their experience of characteristics of the product which have caused problems in the past.

An example of how problems can be avoided arises from one of the author's experiences of running a business supplying made-to-measure loose furniture covers. Where the customer ordered a fabric with a pattern, unless huge quantities of fabric were to be wasted – and prices increased dramatically – there could be no guarantee that the pattern would match wherever there was a seam. Accordingly, the business's terms of trading, set out on the order form which the customer signed, contained a clause bringing this to the customer's attention.

The problem is that the majority of people do not read the documentation they sign, especially where customers are members of the public. The clause is still of benefit, however; the customer who subsequently makes a complaint of this nature usually concedes once the clause – to which they have put their signature signifying their assent – is pointed out to them.

Case study

Alamo Carpet's main supplier, Manufacturing Ltd, use their own documentation not only when dealing with customers but also with their suppliers. Manufacturing Ltd endeavour to buy in supplies of materials used in their manufacturing process on the basis of terms set out on the back of their purchase order form.

This set of terms, unlike those supplied to Alamo Carpets, was devised with the interests in mind of Manufacturing Ltd as buyers.

PURCHASE CONDITIONS

Hereinafter references in these conditions to 'the company' are references to Manufacturing Limited and references to 'the supplier' are references to the person, firm, company or organisation contracting with the company.

1. Delivery
The suppliers shall deliver the goods carriage paid to the delivery address specified by the company.

2. Risk
The goods shall remain at the risk of the seller until delivery has been made to the buyer in accordance with the terms hereof.

3. Delayed Delivery

In the event of late delivery the company shall be entitled at its option to terminate this agreement and reject the goods. In the event that the goods are thereafter wrongfully delivered to the company it shall be the duty of the supplier to arrange collection of the goods forthwith at the expense of the supplier.

4. Specification

In the event of any variation from the specification or description of the goods including any variation in dimensions weight or manner in which the goods are to be packed the company shall have the right to terminate the contract and reject the goods whether or not such variations would affect the market value of the goods.

5. Acceptance of Terms by the Supplier

These terms shall prevail over any terms offered by the supplier.

6. Payment

Payment shall be made at the end of the second month following the month in which goods are delivered.

7. Price

The price(s) stated in this order are firm.

The remaining clauses related to the situation where goods had been specially made for the company, and were concerned with such matters as tooling and the return of any patterns or drawings supplied by the company.

Chapter 8

Contract for the Sale of Goods: Protecting the Buyer

We saw in the case study that, unlike Alamo Carpets, Manufacturing Ltd also use their own documentation when dealing with their suppliers. In practice it is not as common for a buyer to use his own documentation in making a contract to purchase goods as it is for a seller to endeavour to contract on his own terms. This is probably because the Sale of Goods Act, as we have seen, places extensive obligations on the seller for the protection of the buyer, including a trade buyer. Nevertheless, where the buyer is not using his own terms, some of the rules which will otherwise govern the relationship can be a surprise for him.

The standard form documentation sent by Manufacturing Ltd to its suppliers when making purchases, like that sent to its customers, contains clauses which are typical of those encountered in daily business life.

1. Delivery
The suppliers shall deliver the goods carriage paid to the delivery address specified by the company.

This clause is in response to the provision for delivery made by the Sale of Goods Act (see Chapter 6). We noted there how, unless the parties agree otherwise, the place of delivery shall in the normal course of events be the seller's place of business. Clearly this does not accord with the wishes of the buyer in most commercial transactions (as opposed to retail purchases by consumers). Buyers in business expect delivery to be made to them, unless they are buying from cash and carry wholesalers. Suppliers will usually make reference in their literature, often in a price list, to the question of delivery because of the wish to stipulate carriage costs. So a clause which provides for the seller to pay the costs of carriage may contradict a stipulation by the seller that carriage costs will be extra or will be included in the price only where the order is above a given quantity or value.

2.   Risk

The goods shall remain at the risk of the seller until delivery has been made to the buyer in accordance with the terms hereof.

If the goods are damaged or stolen in transit, upon whose shoulders does the loss fall? The law's answer is that the risk of loss or damage to the goods passes with the ownership of the goods. This is probably what the parties would, on reflection, expect the position to be: that the owner of the goods is to bear any loss or damage. However, we have seen earlier that unless a contrary intention is shown by the parties, in a sale of specific goods ownership usually passes not when delivery is made, and the goods are thus in the safe hands of the buyer, but when the agreement is made. Consequently unless the parties make some provision of their own as to the passing of risk, as here, then the goods will be at the buyer's risk even though they are not yet in his possession. If no such provision as to risk is made, the buyer should make sure that his insurance covers the goods from the time ownership passes, not simply when he has them in his possession.

3.   Delayed Delivery

In the event of late delivery the company shall be entitled at its option to terminate this agreement and reject the goods. In the event that the goods are thereafter wrongfully delivered to the company it shall be the duty of the supplier to arrange collection of the goods forthwith at the expense of the supplier.

Late delivery makes life difficult for the buyer, where lack of raw materials or components holds up manufacturing; or the goods are for resale to the buyer's own customers, who are complaining to him about his own consequential late delivery. We have seen earlier that in a contract for the sale of goods where both parties are in business it is likely that late delivery will entitle the buyer to treat the contract as being at an end and, accordingly, to reject the goods. Since the buyer's position is not entirely free of doubt, the draftsman of the contract has endeavoured to reinforce it by spelling out the right to terminate and reject for late delivery.

4. Specification

In the event of any variation from the specification or description of the goods including any variation in dimensions weight or manner in which the goods

*are to be packed the company shall have the right to terminate the contract
and reject the goods whether or not such variations would affect the market
value of the goods.*

This is another example of a clause that may or may not have been
necessary. We have seen how, unless validly excluded, section 13 of the
Sale of Goods Act provides that in a sale by description goods must
correspond with that description, such a term being a condition. In the
past the courts have interpreted widely the word description to include
statements as to the dimensions of the goods and how they are to be
packed.

In one famous case involving the sale of canned fruit the agreement
was that the tins of fruit were to be packed in boxes containing 30. The
total number of tins supplied was correct but a proportion of them
were packed in 24s. This did not affect the value of the produce.
However, the judge held that the way the tins were to be packed formed
part of the description and accordingly there was a breach of
description entitling the buyer to terminate the contract and reject the
goods.

Recently lawyers have had cause to doubt whether the court or
arbitrator would allow a buyer such a powerful remedy for small
variations from description, especially in such matters as packing,
where they did not affect the market value. In the 1970s, in giving
judgement in a case, the House of Lords – for most cases our
highest appellate court – said that a number of older cases about
minor variations from description, including the one involving the tins,
might require reconsideration. The senior judge giving the judgement
of the court was unhappy with the prospect of a relatively minor
deviation in part of the description enabling the buyer to terminate the
contract.

This unease appears to have been picked up by contract draftsmen,
who are attempting to ensure the buyer's right to end the contract if
there is any variation from the seller's description. Is it justifiable for
the buyers to avail themselves, assuming their documentation holds
good, of such a deadly remedy for a minor variation from the seller's
description of the goods? The answer is that there *could* be circumstances in which such a clause would be justified. For example, the
regular supplier could make a minor but repeated deviation which is
sufficient to cause inconvenience to the buyer, the pleas of the buyer to
adhere to the agreement falling upon deaf ears. One of the authors has
had experience of such a situation: a long-term customer, his patience
exhausted by persistent delivery of goods not quite in accordance with

the seller's description, returned a consignment to a supplier who appeared unable to prevent the situation. The supplier's reaction on receipt of the goods was; 'You can't do that!' His attention was drawn to the terms of the agreement.

The supplier had received a jolt in his relationship with the customer. Future consignments were strictly in accordance with the contract.

5. *Acceptance of Terms by the Supplier*
These terms shall prevail over any terms offered by the supplier.

The clause is a bold thrust in the battle of the forms: a bold assertion that the contract is on the buyer's terms. In practice, it is quite likely that the seller's terms will contain a clause to the opposite effect! We have seen that in such a situation the court may seek refuge in applying the rules as to offers and counter offers, holding that where contradictory sets of terms have been flying back and forth between the parties, those prevailing will be the set last tendered without being met with a rejection (whether in the shape of an outright rejection or a counter offer).

Whose terms will prevail must therefore depend on the facts of each individual case.

Implied terms

It is not uncommon for a buyer to expressly recite terms that would be implied into the contract by the Sale of Goods Act. These include the implied terms as to merchantability, that the goods shall correspond with the description, and that the goods shall be fit for a particular purpose which has been made known to the supplier. We have outlined already the obligations imposed by these implied terms.

Since these terms are put into the contract in any case by the Sale of Goods Act, what is the purpose of making them express provisions? It is a fact that many suppliers have never heard of the Sale of Goods Act. While the Act may make suppliers subject to these obligations, it seems more likely that they will comply with them if they know of them! Bigger companies will be aware of their obligations but it is surprising how many small suppliers operate in complete ignorance of their legal rights and duties.

A buyer's documentation may also include an implied term relating to samples. It may be that in the course of a sales demonstration or negotiations a supplier has shown the buyer a product sample. This may be either in lieu of or in addition to any description applied to the goods by the supplier. In a sale by sample the Act implies a term into the contract that the goods shall correspond with the sample in quality. Note that the Act does not say that the goods shall correspond with the sample in every way. Suppose, for example, a toy wholesaler shows a retailer a sample of his new water pistol, available in an attractive range of colours. The retailer will probably not be happy to find he is supplied with three dozen yellow pistols simply because the sample shown to him happened to be that colour. This is why it is often necessary to include a description of the goods where the buyer has been supplied with a sample. In our illustration the contract could specify 'assorted colours', or whatever else is appropriate.

Some other useful clauses

Depending on the nature of the product, it might be necessary to include in the terms clauses covering the following.

Spares. A clause requiring the seller to maintain stocks of spares for a stipulated period of time. This could be a prerequisite where the seller is the only likely source of spares for a particular brand of product, for example, the sole importer.

Tooling. Where the seller is manufacturing items especially for the buyer some additional matters may need to be considered. For example, if tooling is to be specially made, who is to pay for this? If the buyer is to meet the costs, does the contract make clear that this is to be the property of the buyer? What are the arrangements for the return of the tooling to the buyer?

Checklist

The following checklist can serve as a series of starting points for your thoughts. This, and other checklists provided, sets out the principal matters which you should consider, depending on the nature of the contract. Each of these matters is almost certain to have several aspects. The list is not exhaustive: it points to the core features of the majority of contracts of that type; depending on the nature and complexity of any particular transaction, there may be other important matters that require attention.

Contract for the sale of goods

- The parties
- Exclusion or limitation of liability
- Specification/description
- Price
- Payment
- Delivery
- Risk
- *Force majeure*
- Passing of ownership
- Variation
- Guarantee
- Sample
- Rules or implied terms to oust
- Other matters.

Chapter 9

What Might Go Wrong?

With a small everyday transaction, such as the purchase of a newspaper, there is little room for anything to go wrong between the seller and buyer, but once we move up the scale of complexity the opportunities to fall into a legal hole soon appear. The guidelines set out here can usefully be borne in mind when making all but the tiniest, most commonplace contract.

Those of us using the business's existing standard documentation may feel that many of the matters will already have been taken care of by those responsible for drafting the documentation. Such an optimistic assumption may not be well founded.

'We've been using that form without trouble for years.'

One of the authors was asked to conduct a training session on contract law for a household name company. During a break between sessions a member of the management team asked if the author would like to see, out of interest, a copy of one of the company's most important standard contract forms. The company insisted the contract form should be used by suppliers installing or maintaining plant or equipment for the company's manufacturing process at any of its several factories throughout the UK. The author was told that the document was legally watertight, having cost the company 'a fortune' to have it drafted by an eminent barrister. 'That was before my time though, of course', the manager added. 'And how long have you been with the company?' the author asked. The reply came back: 'Just over 15 years'.

The author glanced at the document and there leapt out from the printed page a figure for a sum of money. Drawn by the £ sign in this clause, the author read how, in the event of a failure by the suppliers resulting in disruption of production, the suppliers would be liable to pay fixed compensation of £300 per day – an example of a liquidated damages clause.

It is easy to underestimate the cumulative effects of inflation. This clause was inserted in the mid-1970s, a period during which inflation was rampant and in one particular year hit almost 30 per cent. Nobody in the company had reviewed the document from the time it had been drafted. The author asked himself: 'What is £300 15 years ago worth today?'

The scrutiny was to reveal worse yet to come. The author enquired whether the company's operations had grown over the 15 years. The reply was that the company had opened new factories whose operations were on a much larger scale than the older plants, and had increased several-fold the capacity of most of its existing factories. 'So what might a day's lost production at your biggest factory cost you in profits?' the author asked. 'At a guess I should think about £20,000,' came the reply.

The company's own documentation – devised to protect the company's interests – would, in the event of a breach of contract by the supplier, rob the company of most of the compensation to which it would have been entitled.

Guideline 1. If your business uses standard documentation or incorporates standard terms of trading in its transactions, review those terms from time to time.

Even where the documentation or set of clauses has originally been devised or scrutinised by a legal mind, it could still inflict legal wounds – self-inflicted – on the business at a later date. The law which formed the basis on which the terms were drafted is not static. It is hoped that any change in the law which impinges upon the company's operations will be picked up from a trade or professional journal – if it is reported – by somebody within the company, and will result in a reference to the company's solicitors. But should you rely on that? If a company has the benefit of its own in-house legal experts, presumably its documentation will be subjected to periodic scrutiny by a legal eye, but does the company's solicitor do this?

A business without the benefit of in-house legal expertise could put a note in someone's desk diary, perhaps the company secretary's, reminding him or her to refer the company's documentation to their legal advisers at regular intervals, but that person should not wait until the time for the next check-up should news of a relevant change in the law come to his notice beforehand.

'That's not what I meant!'

All persons involved in the making of contracts should have a large notice pinned up on the wall facing their desk, with the word 'Clarity!' written boldly on it.

Clarity must be in the forefront of your mind at all times when you are involved in any way in the making of a contract. To speak of an 'unclear contract' is a contradiction in terms. The parties may have intended to create a legally binding agreement, but if the contents of that agreement are not clear they will have failed in their endeavours. How can it be otherwise? If the court does not know what the parties have agreed, how can it hold them to it?

Scammell v Ouston (1941)

The plaintiff placed an order with the defendants for a van. The written order stated that the van was to be supplied on 'hire purchase terms'. The order was accepted by the defendants but afterwards they refused to deliver the van and the plaintiff sued for damages for breach of contract. The defendants contended that there was no contract. The case worked its way up to the House of Lords.

The court held in favour of the defendants. As now, there was at that time wide variation in hire purchase terms and it was therefore not clear what the terms would be.

In the Scammel case one of the appeal judges, Lord Wright, said: 'If the words used fail to evince any definite meaning on which the court can safely act, the court has no choice but to say that there is no contract.'

Where the parties, believing they have formed a contract, then act on it, the courts are naturally disinclined to find that in the event no contract was ever made, particularly where one or both of the parties have acted to their detriment. Thus the judge may be pleased to find a source of clarification in the previous dealings of the parties or, if they belong to a particular trade, in a practice of that trade. In such cases the judge will declare the offending clause is only *apparently* vague and uncertain; to one of the parties, however, this apparent vagueness was presumably real enough to pursue the matter through the courts. In making our contract then, we will not leave it to the vagaries of litigation for a court to declare an apparent ambiguity to be capable of clarification.

Guideline 2. The terms of your agreement will be clear.

Certain words in the English language are open to too many interpretations to be of any use to a contract maker. The word 'lucky', used in an old case, is such a word. Ask people what would constitute being lucky and hear the diversity of replies. You will even find that what one person considers to be lucky another considers to be unlucky. Everybody has their own opinion on what amounts to good fortune. Be alert to the use of such words.

'I've left something out!'

Faced with an omission from the contract, the attitude of the court, expressed in cases down the centuries, will be that it is for the parties to make their contract and not for the court to make it for them. The omission may be such that the court will hold there was no concluded agreement, and thus no contract. Or there may be a contract but it will have to function without the clause which one of the parties now wishes he had included.

An apparent exception to this is where the parties have not bothered to state something because it is obvious. It is only an apparent exception to the rule that the court will not make the terms because in such a case the court is not adding a term which the parties have omitted. It is merely giving voice to a term which is in existence; one which is so obvious that the parties did not bother to write or say it. But such cases are rare. If what has not been expressed is so obvious, why are the parties now in heated dispute about whether it was included in the agreement?

Guideline 3. Make sure your agreement is comprehensive.

'I didn't read it!'

Do you read a document before you sign it?

A lawyer will tell you that the majority of his clients, including business people, are all too happy to sign documents without first reading them. This is probably not so where a transaction has been individually negotiated and we are presented with a typed document which is supposed to record what the parties have agreed. Naturally we, or somebody on our behalf, will verify that what is written reflects accurately what has been agreed. But in the hurly burly of day-to-day commercial life we have far less resistance to signing printed pieces of paper, particularly where we are accustomed to them. Also an inducing factor is that a document headed, for example, 'Order Form' or 'Acknowledgement of Order' is less imposing than one headed 'Contract'. It is more likely to strike us that this last has legal consequences.

The courts have adopted a robust attitude towards those of us who, after we have signed a contract, cry that we have not read it. Their attitude is understandable and necessary: signing the document, putting our name to it, is an act by which we declare our assent to the contents. By putting what we have agreed into writing and going through the ceremony of signing the document we are underlining the sanctity of the agreement; we are demonstrating to the world that we intend these matters to be binding upon us and the other party.

L'Estrange v F Graucob Ltd (1934)

The plaintiff wished to buy a cigarette vending machine for her cafe. She signed a written agreement for the purchase of a machine from the defendants. The machine did not work properly and the plaintiff sued the defendants. They pointed to a clause, in small print, which excluded their liability. The plaintiff had not read the document before putting her signature to it, nor was it read over to her. *The court held* that the plaintiff was bound by the written agreement.

If the courts were to allow us to ride free after emphasising the sanctity of the agreement, by crying out that we did not read it, the procedure would be rendered pointless. Where the parties have signed a written agreement they are bound by it whether they have read it or not, and whether they have understood it or not.

It may be different, of course, if the other party misleads us about what the document says in order to induce us to sign it.

> *Guideline 4. Read, and make sure you understand, a written contract before signing it.*

'We've found out we can't do it after all . . .'

It may seem to be stating the obvious when we say: make sure that you will be able to do what you are undertaking in the contract. But if you stop and think about this for a moment, we are all too familiar in our personal and business lives with the person who has promised to do something and then lets us down. And sadly, the party in the wrong often does not seem to be too concerned about his failure. These lax attitudes may stem from two common misconceptions: first, the other party may not realise that he has made a contract and is under a legally binding obligation; or second, the other party feels that it is not his fault that he is unable to meet his promise, that he has done his best, and that this therefore excludes him from any sort of legal responsibility.

What is it that you are promising?

Whether or not the fact that a contracting party has made reasonable efforts is sufficient to discharge his obligations under the contract depends on what he undertook to do in the first place: usually it is not. What was the nature of his promise? Did he undertake to bring about a result? For example, a garage customer complains of 'a drumming sound coming from underneath the car somewhere'. The foreman says they will 'have a look and see what we can do', if the customer will leave the car with them. This probably translates into an obligation to use reasonable skill to discover the source of the noise. But because of the nature of the problem, it is doubtful that the garage staff are undertaking to guarantee that they will make an accurate diagnosis the first time they try. A courier service, on the other hand, which expressly undertakes to deliver a package to the addressee by 9 am the following morning is almost certainly undertaking to bring about a definite result.

Both the courier and the garage must use reasonable skill and exercise reasonable care in carrying out their services and a failure to do so will, in the normal way, amount to a breach of their obligations. In the example of the garage, what they are promising to do amounts to not much more than that: to attempt, using reasonable skill, to discover the cause of the fault by the time the customer comes to collect the car. In the case of the courier service the fact that they have used reasonable skill and taken reasonable care in their efforts to secure delivery by the promised time does not necessarily absolve them from liability if they have failed to do so.

Can the garage guarantee to diagnose the source of the noise by the time the customer comes to collect the car? Probably not – they should beware therefore of appearing to undertake otherwise. This reminds us again of the need for clarity in our dealings.

Be sure that you can achieve what you are promising. If in doubt undertake only that which you know you can do, and express yourself in such a way that the other party is clear about what they are to receive under the agreement.

What is within your control?

Before undertaking contractual obligations, think about what problems *might* arise. For example, where you are undertaking to perform work in the open air your ability to make progress could depend on weather conditions.

This example is a reminder that your ability to fulfil your obligations may depend to a greater or lesser extent on matters which are not completely within your control. What happens if your own suppliers let you down? Good commercial practice and business management may alleviate many of the potential problems. For example, a business that supplies and makes up curtain material for customers may feel confident in guaranteeing to complete an order for made-to-measure curtains if the material chosen by the customer is in stock. If the customer has selected a fabric which then has to be ordered, what would be the shop's position if the suppliers have deleted the item from their range? Or the suppliers find they are unable to obtain the necessary dye to produce the fabric? Probably the shop should take orders for fabric that is not in stock only on the basis that such orders are subject to the fabric being available.

So because of certain events or the failings of other people, you may find it unexpectedly difficult to meet the obligations which you have undertaken to carry out. But since you have chosen to undertake these obligations, presumably because it pays you to do so, the courts take the view that it is for you to exercise judgement, care and expertise in deciding what you can or cannot deliver; the fact that it has turned out more difficult than you envisaged does not allow you to abandon your undertaking. The whole point of making the contract – a legally binding agreement – is to make arrangements certain, so that we may rely on what has been agreed. Accordingly, in contracts where a contracting party's efforts could be subject to matters outside his control, it is common to insert a *force majeure* clause which modifies the party's obligations.

This can be worded in general terms, for example asserting that the party concerned shall not be liable for failure to fulfil his obligations where this is due to circumstances beyond his control. Or the clause may provide that he will not be liable in particular circumstances, eg where there is industrial action. Where particular causes are given, the clause usually makes it clear that these are not exhaustive and that *any* failure due to circumstances beyond the party's control excuses him. The object of these clauses is to release the supplier from liability for damages for non-performance.

A different approach is to provide for the time allowed under the contract to be extended for events beyond the party's control. This has the advantage from the supplier's point of view that he can still fulfil the order and take his profit from the contract.

Very occasionally something happens that makes it not merely more difficult but *impossible* to perform the contract. Here some relief may be available under the legal doctrine of frustration. To a contracting party who is struggling to meet an obligation which is more difficult than he envisaged, this may sound like an avenue of escape. But it is too easy to mislead yourself into believing that your obligations have become impossible to perform. The contracting party should not ask himself: 'Am I able to complete this contract at the agreed price?', but rather: 'Am I able to complete this contract?' – a different matter entirely.

Davis Contractors v Fareham Urban District Council (1956)

The plaintiffs were building contractors who had agreed to build a number of houses for the local authority at a price of £92,000, completion to be within eight months of the contract date. Due primarily to bad weather, the cost of the building work was £17,000 over the contract price.

The court held that although a contract may be said to be frustrated and the parties released from their obligations where it has become physically incapable of performance, this was not the situation here. The question to ask was: 'Has it become impossible to build these houses in eight months?' The question was not: 'Has it become impossible to build these houses in eight months *at this price?*'

There is a further reason why, although events have brought the contract to a halt, few contracting parties are let off the hook by the doctrine of frustration: they cannot show that they are not responsible for what has happened.

Maritime National Fish Ltd v Ocean Trawlers Ltd (1935)

The defendants entered into a contract to hire a trawler for a period of one year, to be used in Canadian waters. They were aware that its use required a licence from the Canadian Minister of Fisheries. In addition to the trawler, the defendants had four other boats. They applied to the Ministry for five licences and were granted only three.

The court held that the contract was not frustrated and the defendants were liable to pay the cost of hire. Although the defendants had not been granted sufficient licences, it was they who had chosen to use the licences for their other boats, rather than using one for the hired trawler.

Guideline 5. Ask yourself: 'Am I sure that I can carry out what I am promising to undertake?'

Guideline 6. Clarify what you are undertaking so that the other party knows exactly what he will receive under the contract.

Litigation – going to court over a dispute – can be one of the most stressful and unpleasant experiences to be encountered. Most of the disputes examined in this book could have been avoided by the parties when making their contracts if they had known what matters to direct their minds to and had made suitable provision for them in their agreement.

Chapter 10

Contract for Services

Case study

On his second day as proprietor of Alamo Carpet Warehouse, Alan Taylor's post brought two letters: another invoice and an item of junk mail. The invoice was again from Manufacturing Ltd and, also again, was for carpet supplied at a newly increased price.

The company sending out the mail shot, unknown to them, had chosen a most propitious moment. The sales letter explained how John Expert's famous seminar 'The Quiet Salesman' would send sales soaring skywards – just what was needed.

As part of Alamo Carpet Warehouse, Alan had inherited Kev. He was the business's only employee, a 19-year-old sales trainee who had been with Alamo for 10 months. To date, Sid Green, Alamo's former proprietor, had given Kev 30 minutes' sales training which, intentionally or not, had left Kev with the impression that to make a sale he had to keep talking. Alan had watched as Kev spent ten minutes talking non-stop to a man who had come in, only to discover that he was asking for directions to the chemists.

Alan looked at John Expert's sales brochure. 'This power-packed one-day seminar demonstrates how body language and listening skills can increase the order value,' he read. 'Numbers are strictly limited. Complete the booking form and return TODAY.'

Alan thought to himself, if I do that, presumably the booking will be on their terms. By running his own business, he was becoming increasingly conscious of the need to consider the contractual implications of what he was doing when he made arrangements for goods or services.

He examined the booking form. The top half looked straightforward enough, requiring him to fill in details as would be expected, relating to which course was required and who would be attending. The lower half of the form set out the 'Booking Terms'.

JOHN EXPERT SEMINARS
Booking Form

To: John Expert Seminars
International House
Midtown
Midshire MX12 2AB

The Quiet Salesman

No. of places required . . . . . (subject enrolment numbers)

EITHER
We agree to pay the course fee on receipt of invoice before the course commences
OR
(If booking within 14 days of the course date) We enclose cheque in the sum of £ . . . .

Employer's name and address . . . .

. . . .

. . . .

TEL . . . .   FAX . . . .

Signed . . . .   Position . . . .

Name of signatory . . . .   Date . . . .

Name(s) of delegates . . . .

. . . .

. . . .

(You may make substitutions for the delegates named at any time and need not notify us of the change.)

Please make cheques payable to John Expert Seminars. A receipt will be issued on payment of the fee.

Booking Terms
1. Substitution
John Expert Seminars reserve the right to substitute an alternative speaker for the speaker named in our literature.

2. Exclusion of Liability
John Expert Seminars shall not be liable for any loss due to

the act or default of any of their servants unless such act or default could have been avoided by the exercise of due care on the part of John Expert Seminars as employer.

3. Publicity
The client consents to John Expert Seminars making known in its promotional literature and otherwise that the client has used the services of the company.

4. Venue
John Expert Seminars reserve the right to substitute an alternative venue for the venue named in our literature.

5. Cancellations
John Expert Seminars reserve the right to cancel the course due to insufficient enrolments in the event of which monies paid shall be returned but no further liability shall attach to John Expert Seminars.

6. Cancellation by the Client
No cancellations may be made by the client within 10 working days of the commencement of the course. In the event of cancellation made in writing by the client and received earlier than 10 working days before the commencement of the course 50 per cent of the course fee together with VAT shall be payable to John Expert Seminars. In the event that a delegate fails to attend the course no refund of fee shall be payable nor transfer to another course permitted.

A contract by one person undertaking to carry out work for another is very different from a contract for the sale of goods. The manager of a business whose product is a service will deal with different problems from those of the manager of a business which is based on a physical, tangible product. Quality control is more difficult if you are supplying a service for you can only be as good as the people who work for you. It is easier to manufacture that well-known hypothetical product the widget in its thousands, each uniform and perfect, than to provide services of uniform quality. Even if you have attracted and recruited the best people, they can still go through a bad patch in their marriage or 'take to the bottle'!

The sales people working for the service-based business will also tell you that it is often more difficult to *sell* a service. With a manufactured product the potential customer can view a sample and see how attractive and desirable it is, they can feel the quality, they can view the product functioning. But when we commit ourselves to buying services, it is much more uncertain what we will receive; for example, a bank's services will have to be described to the potential customer. There is a greater element of trust when buying services. These differences between services and physical products draw attention to particular considerations when making the contract for services.

Contracts of employment

A contract for services must be distinguished from a contract of employment. Under both types a person is performing work on behalf of another in return for a consideration, but the person performing work under a contract for services is not an employee. Confusingly, the traditional lawyers' term for a contract of employment is a 'contract *of* service'. A contract of employment is an example of a specialised type of contract which, because of its importance forms a branch of law all of its own, the law of employment, and is thus outside the scope of this book. However, it is important for us to be able to distinguish a person performing work under a contract for services (what the law calls an 'independent contractor') from one performing work under a contract of employment. This is because there falls upon both parties to the contract of employment a range of obligations and duties imposed by Parliament and the courts, with the employer shouldering the greater part of this burden. The window cleaner who calls at your home or office from time to time is not your employee and therefore does not enjoy the benefits of employment protection provisions such as the right not to be unfairly dismissed, the right of compensation for redundancy, maternity rights, etc. And you are likely to receive some very funny looks if you attempt to deduct income tax under PAYE from the payment you make to your window cleaner!

In most instances it will be obvious that the contract is a contract of employment, but occasionally it is difficult, if not impossible, to draw the line. This is especially so where in reality the relationship is that of employer and employee but it suits both parties to cloak this relationship – for the employer to treat the employee as a self-employed person. The employer may hope to avoid the obligations placed upon him by employment protection legislation, and the employee probably views the tax treatment of the self-employed as more favourable.

The courts have devised a battery of tests over the years which they use to determine whether in a particular instance the parties are bound by a contract of employment or a contract for services. The traditional test has been the *control test*. The courts have taken the view that a person working under a contract for services (eg the self-employed painter who contracts to paint your property) is told what to do (eg 'paint the front') but not *how* to do it. An employee, by contrast, is told by his employer both what to do and how to do it (eg 'paint the front; use this brush and start at the top'). The control test falls down when it applies to skilled employees, especially professional people such as surgeons, where the employer (eg the hospital management board) does not have the skill to direct how the employee carries out his duties.

One useful test is to ask if the person concerned has the characteristic signs of self-employment, eg does he keep a set of books? But none of the tests on its own is conclusive. Indeed, in one particular case an outspoken judge, having reviewed the tests available and applied them to the facts of the case, is reported to have said that he might as well spin a coin to decide the outcome, which is not a comment likely to induce confidence in litigants coming to the court – although it is probably a fair reflection of what is going on in the judicial mind in a percentage of cases.

Some familiar contracts

Some types of contract for the supply of services in business present particular problems. These contracts include where one party is to act as an agent for the other, where one party is to act as a distributor, and where one party is to provide the services of a consultant. We shall look briefly at these types later in this chapter.

The Supply of Goods and Services Act

We have seen how, in a contract for the sale of goods, Parliament endeavours to protect the recipient of the goods by implying terms into the contract to which the parties may otherwise not have expressly agreed. These included terms as to merchantability, fitness for particular purpose, and compliance with description. Similarly, in a contract for the supply of services Parliament implies terms into a contract in an endeavour to establish minimum standards which the recipient of the services can expect to receive under the contract. The Act does not apply to every type of service supplied by a business; for example, the services of a lawyer in court are expressly excluded! However, it endeavours to deal with the most common problems, by providing answers to the following questions:

1. What is to be the standard of the services provided?
2. How long does the supplier have to complete the work?
3. What is to be the price payable?

The standard of the services

The Act implies a term into the contract that the supplier will carry out the services using reasonable skill and taking reasonable care. This does not seem a particularly onerous obligation to meet, representing the standard which we would expect to receive under a contract for services.

Time for completion

It is not uncommon for the parties to leave open the date for completion of the services; for some types of work it may be difficult to gauge exactly how long the work will take. Where the contract is silent as to a completion date the Act implies a term that the services shall be rendered within a reasonable time.

What is the position where the services are not completed on time? The decisions of the courts seem to indicate that failure to complete on time does not entitle the other party to treat the contract as being at an end, except where it was clear when the contract was made that completion by the date specified was essential. In practice, when services are not completed on time the customer will want to know when he *can* expect completion. If this new date is also broken, is the customer still bound by the contract? The supplier is not entitled to go on indefinitely breaking promises as to the completion date. After a reasonable time the customer can give notice to him that unless the services are completed within the time he has specified in the notice, the buyer will treat the contract as being at an end.

The price payable

This is another term which in a contract for services is very often left open, much more so than in a contract for the sale of goods. Just as the question of a completion date is often left open because of the problem of gauging how long the work will take, so too with the question of cost. This can cause painful shocks – the emergency plumber called out to unblock a drain presents a bill far beyond what the customer would have expected. Does the customer have to pay? If the plumber and his customer did not agree how the bill should be arrived at when he agreed to undertake the work, then the customer, relying on a term implied by the Act, need pay only what is reasonable in all the circumstances.

Particular considerations of the contract for services

The booking form provided by John Expert Seminars for Alan Taylor to complete in our case study attempts to deal with some of the particular considerations in making a contract for services.

1. Substitution
John Expert Seminars reserve the right to substitute an alternative speaker for the speaker named in our literature.

The sales leaflet sent to prospective clients contained a full colour picture of John Expert, who has written numerous books on sales technique, is consultant to several multinationals, and who has conducted his seminars to widespread acclaim throughout Europe and North America.

The general rule provided by the law of contract is that where services are contracted for they do not have to be performed by a named individual unless either the agreement provides for this, or looking at all the circumstances, it must have been contemplated by the parties that the services would have to be performed by that particular person. In many contracts under which services are to be performed, it would be irrelevant to the recipient of the services which of his fellow human beings actually carries out the work; for example, in a contract to have the windows cleaned regularly by Dazzle Cleaning Services the customer company will not know or care whether it will be Mick or John or Darren who comes to clean them. On the other hand, if an opera house contracts for a world famous soprano to sing the lead in its new opera, clearly neither the opera house nor its patrons expect the soprano to send along her mother to do a turn in her place while she goes off to perform under a more lucrative contract. The task of performance cannot be delegated to another if the customer can show that they entered into the contract because John Expert would be conducting the seminar and they have confidence in him personally, his skills and his abilities.

Thus, where a business puts emphasis in its marketing on the individual qualities of the person who is to perform the services, clearly it is prudent to attempt to make express provision in the contract for those services to be provided by an alternative. It is possible that such a clause could be caught by the provisions of the Unfair Contract Terms Act, where it is contained in a standard form contract or a consumer contract. As we have mentioned earlier, sometimes a clause in a contract will attempt to permit a party to render performance of the contract different from that which the other party might reasonably expect. A common example is where the terms of booking for a package holiday permit the tour operator to change the hotel. If, instead of the 5-star Hotel Grand described in the brochure, they put the client into the 1-star Hotel Cheapo, this would be a performance of the contract different from that which the client might reasonably expect. (He might have expected a transfer to another 5-star hotel or perhaps even to a 4-star hotel, but not the Hotel Cheapo.) Under the Act a clause enabling one of the parties to render a performance different from that expected, as in clause 1 here, is valid only to the extent that it is fair and reasonable.

2. Exclusion of Liability

John Expert Seminars shall not be liable for any loss due to the act or default of any of their servants unless such act or default could have been avoided by the exercise of due care on the part of John Expert Seminars as employer.

John Expert's exclusion clause attempts to limit liability for harm caused by employees, referred to here by the lawyers' more traditional term 'servants'.

The reaction of many non-lawyers to a clause of this type is along the lines: 'But surely the employer is not liable anyway for what the employee has done. It's not the boss that's done it. The boss shouldn't be liable for what somebody else has done.'

We mentioned earlier, in Chapter 5, a branch of the law concerned with providing compensation where one person causes harm to another, such as injury to the person, to their good name, or to their property: the law of torts. As a general legal principle, people are liable for their own wrongs and not for what others do, but there are exceptions, one being that an employer is liable for the torts committed by his employees in the course of their employment.

If one of John Expert's catering assistants, providing refreshments during a break, is not paying attention to what he is doing and spills boiling coffee over a delegate, John Expert will be liable.

A clause attempting to limit liability for the acts of employees might be found in any contract – in a contract for the sale of goods a delivery driver might drop the goods on the customer's toes. But in a contract to provide services there is often greater opportunity for the acts of employees to cause harm to customers, so here such a clause is more common (and perhaps even more so in a contract for services and goods, a type of contract we shall be looking at in Chapter 12).

In attempting to insert such a clause, two points in particular need to be borne in mind. First, a business cannot exclude liability for personal injury caused by negligence. John Expert cannot exclude liability if his catering assistant doesn't look where he is going and scalds a delegate by spilling coffee over him.

Second, an attempt to exclude liability for other loss, eg damage to the delegate's suit caused by the hot coffee, will be valid only to the extent, again, that it is fair and reasonable.

3. *Publicity*
The client consents to John Expert Seminars making known in its promotional literature and otherwise that the client has used the services of the company.

As it is often more difficult to sell a service because the customer has to take on trust what he is to receive, the reputation of the business is of even more importance. It is not uncommon for a company whose product is a professional service to trumpet in their marketing that prestigious names have made use of their services. John Expert's clause 3 secures permission to do so.

The client company may not like to see in the brochure that its name is included in a list of those who have used John Expert's services. The client may feel that its use of these services is confidential, that it does not want its customers to know that its sales force has been trained in what the customers may regard as high pressure sales techniques. If the client complains the business will have to weigh commercial considerations against legal considerations. Where the complainant is a former client who no longer uses the business's services, John Expert may choose to refer the complainant to the booking terms to which he assented. If the complainant is a current client, he may instead express his regret and undertake not to use the client's name in future promotional literature. Presumably, in the first situation, any qualms of conscience John Expert may have over using the name of a company or person who is unhappy about it will be eased by the knowledge that they signed their assent to a contract containing a clause authorising such use.

A contract to act as an agent

An agent is somebody who, in law, has the power to act on behalf of another, by entering into contracts that bind that other person. The person for whom the agent acts is the principal. The most common use of an agent is to act as a representative for the purpose of making sales. In practice, many business people use the term agent loosely, without being aware of its legal significance.

Businesses which make routine use of agents may have their own standard form agency agreement; a professional agent such as a sales agent will probably also use his own standard documentation, which may have been devised and recommended by his own professional association.

In a contract to appoint an agent, the following matters should be borne in mind:

1. What is to be the extent of the agent's authority? For example, is the agent to have the authority to agree with customers of the principal any variation in price? Is he to have authority to agree pre-contract amendments to the principal's standard terms? Note, however, that if the agent agrees something which is outside his actual authority, but outsiders could reasonably expect him to have that power, the principal will be bound by what the agent has agreed. The agent would, however, be liable to the principal for breach of his agency contract.

2. In the geographical area in which the agent represents the principal, is he to be the sole agent? Can the principal himself make sales to customers? If so, does the agent receive commission?

3. How is the agent's remuneration to be calculated? It is common for sales agents to be paid on the basis of results, receiving a commission on sales. At what intervals is this to be paid? At what stage in the transaction conducted by the agent does remuneration for the transaction become payable – is it when the agent introduces a person willing and able to buy, when the order is placed, or when the transaction is completed? If the agent has an exclusive territory, what is the position where the enquiry is generated by an agent outside that territory? This could happen for example where another agent's customer suggests the name of a potential customer to that agent, who then passes it on. Is the agent's commission to be lost in the event of cancellation by the customer? Automatic debiting of commission may give rise to a justified grievance where the cancellation is due to the default of the company, eg the customer has cancelled because of late delivery, and is unconnected with the agent's performance of his duties.

4. Is the agent permitted to represent other principals whose products may be in competition with your products? In some instances it is only by offering a range of products from competing suppliers that the agent is able to function. This is often the case with professional agents who are used by manufacturers and importers to call on wholesalers and retailers

– the agent can interest retailers in his wares because he is able to offer a range from different manufacturers.

Many small businesses in particular seem happy to create the contractual relationship of principal and agent by the briefest of letters, and only turn their attention to some of the above matters when a dispute arises.

A sale arranged by an agent is in fact made between the person on whose behalf the agent acts, the principal, and the customer; the goods or services are not bought from the agent but from the person for whom the agent acts. It follows that since the goods are sold by the principal, the buyer's contractual remedies are against the principal and not against the agent. For example, if the goods are defective and in breach of the terms implied by the Sale of Goods Act, it will be the principal and not the agent who is liable.

Since the term agency is often used by business people who are unaware of its legal meaning, the business may purport to offer an agency when in fact it should more properly be called a distributorship.

A contract to act as a distributor

A distributor is in essence a stock holder. When a sale is made by a distributor, in contrast to that made by an agent, the customer is the customer of the distributor. The sale is by the distributor to the customer and it follows from this that responsibilities under the contract of sale, including the terms implied for the protection of the buyer by the Sale of Goods Act, fall upon the distributor. Where the goods are defective the distributor will in turn have his remedy against his own supplier, assuming that his supplier has not excluded liability. If the distributor is selling on to consumers, as we have seen, he cannot exclude his liability for goods which are unmerchantable or not as described. The burden for defective goods may thus, depending on the terms of the supplier/distributor contract, fall upon those who sell to consumers rather than their suppliers: a factor to take into account when assessing prices to be charged to the consumer. This situation can arise not just in the case of distributors; exclusion clauses in wholesalers' and manufacturers' terms may similarly have the effect of leaving responsibility for breaches of the Sale of Goods Act with the retailer.

For the supplier, the other main benefit of a distributorship arrangement is that he has to deal with far fewer entities (his distributors) rather than all the customers for his product.

Agreements in restraint of trade

Some of the considerations raised by agency agreements are relevant also to agreements for distributorships, including whether the distributor is to have an exclusive territory and whether he is to be allowed to represent others whose products compete with the products of your business. On this last point the legal position is, however, rather different – and more problematic – from that of an agency.

A case came before the courts in modern times in which one of the parties had agreed, among other matters, to purchase supplies of petrol for resale only from the other party. The court held that such a 'solus' agreement could be caught by the rules on restraint of trade. A clause in restraint of trade is one by which the person undertakes to restrict in the future who he will do business with or the manner in which he will do business. Such a clause could be declared by the court to be void, that is to say, devoid of legal effect. In our free enterprise society such clauses are regarded as injurious to society as a whole. To be valid, a clause of this type must be drafted in such a way that the restriction is no wider than is reasonably necessary to protect the party's legitimate interests.

Note also that an agreement which includes restrictions as to from whom, or to whom, goods are to be supplied may be caught by the provisions of the *Restrictive Trade Practices Act*. The Act applies to certain restrictive agreements; an agreement which falls within the Act must be registered with the Office of Fair Trading, and the Restrictive Practices Court may declare the agreement void. Where solicitors are engaged in drafting agreements that could be caught by the Act they will frequently seek the guidance of the OFT on whether the clause would be valid.

Particular considerations of the distributorship agreement

Because there will be a sale of goods by the supplier to the distributor, the contract between them will have to deal with the usual matters raised by a contract for the sale of goods. In the case of a distributorship agreement you should also consider the following:

1. Is there to be a requirement that the distributor should carry minimum stocks or, put another way, an obligation on the distributor to make a minimum purchase over a given period? This obligation may be one of the core benefits of a distributorship agreement for the supplier. The distributor who has made such an undertaking has good cause to be active in his attempts to sell the product.

2. Does the supplier undertake to support the distributor in terms of promotional material and advertising? This will be more important to the distributor who has agreed to a minimum stockholding clause. For his part, the supplier may feel that the distributor should contribute towards the cost of advertising.

    The clause which provides for support by the supplier should define what the distributor can expect. Promotional materials, such as point of sale aids, could be specified; for example, the supplier undertakes to provide a display stand. Defining the extent to which the supplier is to undertake advertising is more difficult – one solution is to provide that £x will be expended for y volume of turnover. For example, the supplier undertakes to allocate a given percentage of the sales turnover achieved by the distributor in any one financial year.

    Does the distributor have an obligation to undertake publicity? Will this require the prior approval of the supplier?
3. Although the customers for the goods will be the customers of the distributor, nevertheless the supplier's reputation attaches to the goods. Should the agreement require the distributor to undertake efficient after-sales servicing? Should he be required to maintain stocks of spares?

Consultancy agreements

The use by firms of outside consultants has increased enormously in recent years, due in part at least to the fact that the numbers of consultants have also increased. It is especially common in the fields of business management, marketing and product research and development.

The core of most consultancy services consists of giving professional advice. They usually present their clients with their own standard form contract, although some, usually one-person practitioners, may leave matters to an exchange of letters, which is surprising bearing in mind that these are professional people.

Confidentiality

Most consultants in the process of their work will receive information about the operations and plans of the business which could be of commercial benefit to the business's competitors. A part of the law of torts does in fact make it actionable – the aggrieved party may sue the wrongdoer – for a person to disclose without authority information which has been given to him in circumstances which make it clear that the material was confidential. However, this is a little used area of the law of torts and its exact limits are not well defined. The agreement between the parties should therefore include a clause along the lines that the consultant will not, without the prior written permission of the client, disclose to others information appertaining to the client, other than information which is already in the public domain.

Related to this would be a clause requiring the consultant, after the completion of his work for the client, not to make his services available to competitors. The use of the consultant's services has been for the purpose of developing the company's business to give it a competitive edge. If the consultant does the same for a competitor the advantage to the first client will have been lost.

Such a clause requires most careful wording, however, because it could be another example of restraint of trade. We have seen that a clause deemed by the courts to be in restraint of trade could be declared void if it is wider than is necessary. (It is increasingly common for a clause of this type to be inserted by employers into contracts of employment, particularly for employees with technical knowledge or who have contact with customers.)

In deciding whether the clause is wider than is reasonably necessary to protect the party's legitimate interests the courts look at two aspects:

(a)   how long the restriction is to last; and
(b)   the geographical area covered by the restraint.

If the scope of the clause is drafted too widely, the court will not cut down the clause to what is reasonably necessary and then enforce it to that extent; it will strike out the clause altogether. The party relying on it will then be left entirely without its protection. For example, if the clause restricts a consultant from working for a competitor for two years and the court comes to the view that it would be reasonably necessary to restrain the consultant for only one year, it will not rewrite the clause and order compliance with it for a period of one year; it will simply strike out the clause, leaving that consultant free to work for a competitor immediately. It is therefore better to err on the side of caution, so that the restraint is clearly reasonable.

In order to reinforce the confidential nature of the work another clause could require the consultant on termination of the work, or on prior request, to return to the client all documentation and other materials obtained by the consultant from the client.

Patent rights

Spell out in the consultancy contract the position on patent and similar rights if there is any possibility of them arising. Are these rights to vest in the client? Who undertakes to carry out the procedures, eg patent registration, necessary to afford the relevant legal protection?

Checklist

The following points should be considered when drawing up a contract for services. Remember that each of them is almost certain to have several aspects:

- The parties
- Exclusion or limitation of liability
- Price
- Payment
- Duration/completion date
- Description of services
- Arbitration
- Guarantee
- *Force majeure*
- Variation
- Rules or implied terms to oust
- Other matters.

Chapter 11

Tactics

Most of a business's customers and suppliers are honest and reasonable people. However, a percentage of those we have to deal with need careful handling; for example, the customer whose past complaints have given us cause to doubt their integrity, or someone in the trade who has a reputation for dubious practices. When dealing with such people it is particularly useful to know your legal position and what options it might be prudent for you to adopt.

In the first part of this chapter we look at some situations that can arise in business, in which the other side could cause a headache for us. In the second part we look at some tactics which it may be useful to employ, even if all your customers and suppliers are honest, decent and truthful. They might help you to look after your interests.

How to avoid some headaches

You may recognise from your own experiences some of the following situations.

'We don't want to do business with him.'

From time to time we all come across some individual or firm we do not want to become embroiled with; perhaps the customer would give us too much aggravation, his demands being out of proportion to the benefit we would get from the deal. Unfortunately, often it will only become obvious that we don't wish to deal with this person when we have gone some way down the road with him. It is therefore useful to know at what stage the transaction becomes binding upon us. As we have seen earlier, this is generally the point at which the party to whom an offer has been made communicates that he is accepting. If it is you who has made the offer, the statement of terms, the other party will make an acceptance of that offer, so whether and when the transaction becomes binding is now in their hands; they make it so by communicating their acceptance.

If you have decided you do not want to do business with the other party, don't make an offer. Be sure that what you are saying or writing does not amount to a statement of terms which is capable of being accepted.

If, after an offer has been made, you decide you would prefer not to do business with the other party, the general rule is that an offer can be withdrawn at any time up until acceptance.

Bear in mind, however, when contemplating withdrawing an offer the post rule that we looked at in Chapter 3. You will recall that this rule lays down that where it is reasonable to use the post, a letter of acceptance is deemed to be communicated to the offeror when the letter is put into the post. If in the terms of your offer you have not ousted this rule, then it is possible that the other party has already made a valid acceptance which you have not yet received.

It is not enough to decide to withdraw your offer: revocation of an offer has no validity unless and until it is made known to the offeree. And here is a legal snare into which the unwary will stroll: the post rule does not apply to letters withdrawing offers. A letter accepting an offer is deemed to be communicated when posted: but not so a letter revoking the offer! An example will show what the consequences of this could be. Supplier Ltd makes an offer to Buyer Ltd, then writes on the 8th to withdraw it, the letter being received on the 10th. In the meantime, Buyer posted a letter of acceptance on the 9th. Result: a contract binding both parties came into being on the 9th. Another good reason for making it clear in the terms of your offer that the post rules are ousted.

Byrne & Co v Van Tienhoven & Co (1880)

The defendants offered to sell the plaintiffs 1000 boxes of tin plates, then on 8th October posted a letter revoking the offer. The plaintiffs received this letter in New York on 20th October but, in the mean time, had telegraphed an acceptance on 11th October.

The court held that there was a binding contract made on 11th October. The defendants were liable in damages.

This case brings home a number of lessons. First, note that there was a contract here even though at the time, according to the court, the contract was concluded, one of the two parties did not intend to make the contract. The court held that the contract came into being some days after the offeror had posted a letter withdrawing the offer. Byrne's case is a reminder that the test of agreement is *not*: 'Did the parties intend to make an agreement?'

Second, the post rule (that a letter of acceptance is deemed to be communicated when it is put into the post) was held to apply to telegrams. Thus the defendant's offer was validly accepted when the plaintiffs telegraphed their acceptance on 11th October, *three days after* the letter withdrawing the offer had been sent. Remember, the post rule does not apply to letters withdrawing offers, only to letters, telegrams or telemessages which accept them.

Finally, let us suppose that after the defendants had sent the letter withdrawing the offer, they had then proceeded to sell the tin plates to a third party – a likely possibility; indeed, the chance to sell to a third party is probably the commonest reason for withdrawing an offer from the original offeree. In our experience, many sellers believe that if, after offering to sell goods to *x*, they then sell them to *y*, that puts an end to the matter as far as *x* is concerned. It does not. An offer continues to be operative unless, as we have seen, its withdrawal is communicated to the offeree. We stress that, having made an offer, by putting yourself in a position where you cannot perform the offer, such as selling the goods to a third party, does not of itself terminate the offer.

Of course, if the offeree learns of the sale to a third party, this would amount to notice of revocation and a purported acceptance after learning of the sale would be invalid. In one case *A* offered to sell property to *B*, then sold it to *C*. *B* learned of the sale from *D*, and then attempted to 'accept' the offer, but the court held that *B* had been notified of the revocation even though the offeror himself had not done the communicating. On the other hand, if *B* had not learned of the sale to *C* and had accepted in ignorance of it, there would have been a valid acceptance by him and a contract made with *A*, who would then have been in breach as he would have been unable to convey the property to *B*.

'They said they would keep the offer open.'

When an offer has been made you may need breathing space, for all manner of reasons, before deciding whether or not to accept. You may request the other party to allow you *x* number of days' grace before coming to your decision; you ask them to keep the offer open. Perhaps you then go away and expend money and effort on researching the market; or you take up the time of your colleagues in assessing whether your business has the capacity to meet the obligations; or you seek – and pay for – professional advice in the matter. You have expended time, thought, energy, money, and you are about to reach a decision when the other party informs you that they have withdrawn the offer.

Your response naturally will be: 'But you gave us x days to think about it and we relied upon that!' The chances are that you will write the matter off and chalk it up to experience. If you consult your solicitors, unless the sums involved are considerable, almost certainly their advice will be to take the matter no further. It is not an uncommon situation, especially in particular trades; the other party may have had any number of likely fishes before which he was dangling the hook that one of them would bite upon.

Where you are complaining that the other party has not kept the offer open, you are seeking to hold that party to a promise. This takes us back to elementary contract law: how do we make a promise binding? We make it part of a contract. To do that we must show the presence of the three essential ingredients: agreement, intention to create legal relations, and consideration. What is missing in our illustration is consideration.

Therefore if you wish to have time to consider and want to avoid fruitless effort and expenditure considering an offer which may be aborted, you should:

- ask the other party to agree to keep the offer open; and
- offer something in return.

This consideration that you will be giving is, of course, not the same consideration they will be receiving if both parties go ahead with the main deal. In fact, if the other party agrees to keep the offer open in return for consideration you are then creating a separate contract. The party who made the original offer is now under a legal obligation to keep that offer open. That party is said to have granted an *option*. You are not, of course, under an obligation to accept the offer. We thus have a situation where one side is legally bound and the other is not. If the main deal goes ahead, the parties will have made two contracts.

We have seen earlier that consideration may be something of very small monetary value; if the other party agrees to take some token payment such as £1 for his promise to keep the offer open, this will serve our purpose. If he then attempts to withdraw the offer before the agreed time limit has expired, he will find himself in breach of contract.

One other way of dealing with the problem, instead of giving consideration for the promise to keep the offer open, is to put the promise in a deed. You saw in Chapter 3 that there is no requirement for consideration where the parties use this medium instead of an ordinary written or oral contract. This method is often used in offers to sell land.

'They want to cancel.'

In ordinary contract law the agreement becomes binding when it is made and it is not necessary for money to change hands to make an agreed sale binding on the buyer. However, most members of the public and, unfortunately, many business people, suffer from the delusion that without payment of a deposit the agreement is not binding and they are therefore free to opt out of the sale. Since the buyer has made a legally binding agreement, they do not have a general right under the law to 'cancel' the agreement; nevertheless, payment of a deposit often firms up the sale and deters purported cancellation by the buyer for fear of forfeiting the deposit.

Within the last decade or so a flood of consumer advice has become freely available to the public via television programmes, local authority advice centres, and magazine articles, responding to a growing interest in consumer rights. Many businesses dealing with the public have discovered that a percentage of their customers believe that consumer law enables them to carry on as if they had no obligations themselves under the agreement and that all the obligations are on one side. Very often these customers are the most vociferous and unreasonable. They may have picked up some half-understood consumer law provisions, but remain blissfully ignorant of the law of contract.

Such consumers may have to be reminded that the sale is a contract and that, as such, the agreement is subject not only to the provisions of consumer law but also to the law of contract. This lack of understanding of the law of contract reveals itself in particular over the question of cancellation. Consumers have only very restricted rights of cancellation; primarily, in some circumstances where credit is being granted to them or they are buying goods at home. There is, however, a widespread erroneous belief among consumers that they have the right to 'cancel' *any* agreement after they have made it, and at any time. This cavalier attitude towards cancellations is also to be met in some business people.

In practice many businesses will grin and bear a purported cancellation on the basis that while it is all very well to insist upon strict legal rights, commercial sense says that the customer who is coerced into continuing with an agreement may cause more aggravation than they are worth. And a co-operative response on one occasion may result in business emanating from that customer at some time in the future.

Sometimes a purported cancellation can have serious consequences for the business, for example where goods are being made to the customer's specification. We mentioned earlier that one of the authors was a partner in a business making up and supplying tailor-made loose covers for lounge suites. Their method of working was that the customer would select a particular fabric and shade and the company's representative would individually measure the suite. Up to this point a cancellation would result only in a waste of the time that had been put in to the transaction and the transport costs to the customer's premises to measure the suite. However, once the work in hand had reached the stage of cutting out the fabric, the point of no return had been passed, because clearly the chances of another customer having an identical suite and requiring the same fabric in the same colourway were a million to one. It was at this stage that a cancellation would result in a loss to the business of the not inconsiderable costs of the fabric, as well as the labour costs to date. When devising the business's documentation (in this case an order form) it was therefore decided to spell out to the customer that cancellation could not be accepted by the suppliers.

Note that this is an example of the contract reciting what is in fact the existing legal position. The example demonstrates that there may be good reasons for this. First, the customer may not be aware of the position; second, by reciting the position of the parties as a term of the agreement, one which the other party has signed, it firms up that party's adherence to the provision.

It is true that the other party will discover the legal position when and if they consult their solicitors, but by this time they may already have done the damage; suffering a misconception as to their legal position, they have broken the contract. Where there is a breach of contract the innocent party has the remedies provided by law, but it is better to do what you can from the outset to minimise the risk of the other party failing to carry out the agreement. If nothing else, you may save on legal fees.

Looking after your interests

You may be pleased to avail yourself of the following tactics at some time or other.

To lie low and say nothing

When you are endeavouring to pull off a deal, naturally you will say things to persuade the other party to enter into the transaction. Naturally, you will not allow your enthusiasm and eagerness to tempt you into making or writing statements which are false. However, perhaps others who are acting on your behalf may make the occasional, or not so occasional, lapse – eg the sales representative eager to secure a commission bonus. If you say or write things which you know to be false in order to persuade the other party to do the deal you are exposing yourself to liability for misrepresentation (see Chapter 5). Indeed, it is not even necessary for the other party to prove that you knew the falsity of what has fallen from your lips or your word processor; the contract might be set aside even if you thought the statement was true.

While, during the course of negotiations, you have to say or write things, there may also be moments when you would prefer to remain quiet. As a general rule, this is a contracting party's prerogative. In most contractual relationships there is no duty on one party to disclose matters to the other that affect the other's interests. Even today for any person or business entering into a contract the byword should be 'Beware!'

One important exception to this concerns insurance. Taking out insurance is an example of making a contract to which a specialised body of law applies. There is a duty on one of the parties, the proposer, to make known to the other, the insurer, all the matters that a reasonable and prudent insurer would want to take into account. This duty, of which most people are unaware, is broken in a large percentage of insurance transactions; and never comes to light either because no claim is made under the policy or those made are not for large sums. Many non-lawyers seem unaware of this duty to disclose; it should be borne in mind next time you are taking out – or renewing – any kind of insurance. Failure to disclose makes the contract voidable at the option of the insurers; they are entitled to set it aside and not pay out a claim made under the policy.

To get rid of a clause you do not like

The increase in recent years in the use of standard form contracts brings us face to face with clauses that are not to our liking. Perhaps you are about to place an order for materials with a new supplier. Before signing you duly read the company's standard form agreement – there, at clause 12, is a provision that sticks in your throat.

If you were to strike through the offending clause, initial same, and post the amended document back to the company, this may look like an acceptance but it is in fact a counter offer (see Chapter 3). You will recall that you make a counter offer where you attempt to vary the terms of an offer that has been made to you. If somebody in the offices of Nasty Terms Limited rings or writes to say 'You can't do that', perhaps your bargaining power is so good that you are able to dictate that the business will be done on your terms or not at all. If this is not the case, then you will have to think again as to whether you can live with the clause. But your altered documentation may go through without them bothering about it and once there has been an acceptance the terms of the contract will be the amended terms. A problem could arise, however, if the other side does not spot the alteration. We have seen earlier that if one party makes a mistake about a sufficiently important matter and the other party knows or must have known they had made the mistake, the court may intervene. To avoid that problem, you should make reasonable efforts to bring the alteration to their attention.

Brogden v Metropolitan Railway (1877)

This is a case dating from the days of private railways. Brogden, a coal merchant, had been negotiating terms with the railway company for the supply of coal. The company's agent, who was conducting negotiations for the railway, sent a draft agreement to Brogden. On receiving it, Brogden made an amendment to the draft, signed it, wrote on it 'approved', and returned it. No further communication was received from the agent, who had placed the draft in his desk. Neither the agent nor anyone else signed the draft on behalf of the company. Some coal was subsequently supplied by Brogden to the company but a dispute arose between the parties and Brogden refused to make further supplies, contending that there was no contract under which he was obliged to do so.

The court held (1) that return by Brogden of the draft signed and marked approved was *not* an acceptance of the terms set out but was, in the light of his amendment, a counter offer; (2) that although no express communication of acceptance of the counter offer was made, acceptance can be inferred from conduct; and (3) that a contract came into being at the latest when the company took delivery of coal from Brogden, acceptance of his counter offer being inferred from their conduct in so taking delivery.

Where you are dealing face to face with a representative of the other party, it is likely you will be met with the response that the company will not deviate from its standard terms. Faced with this situation, one of the authors pointed out to a reluctant sales representative that with the documentation remaining as it was the author could not proceed with the deal and the representative would lose his commission. Back came the reply: 'Oh, go on then – I don't suppose anybody will care.'

The offending clause was duly struck through, the amendment initialled by both the author and the representative. Provided the person representing the other contracting party has ostensible authority to agree amendments, the contract will be made on the terms of the counter offer.

Chapter 12

Contract for Work and Materials

Case study

A representative from a burglar alarm company went to survey Alamo Carpet's premises on Wednesday. On Friday the representative, Nick, was back again.

'You received our quotation did you, Mr Taylor?' said Nick.

'I just had a quick look at it,' said Alan. 'I haven't had time to think about it yet.'

Nick made no reply. Nick had also been on John Expert's sales course and had learnt that the salesperson's secret weapon was silence; he was giving Alan time to 'think about it'. Alan wondered why they were just standing there looking at one another.

After 20 seconds Nick said, 'Is there anything else you'd like to think about?'

Alan picked up from his desk the letter that he had received that morning; he read again:

Dear Mr Taylor,

QUOTATION

We now have pleasure in supplying our quotation as follows:

Address of Premises: 13–15 Eastern Road
Midtown
Midshire

Specification: SCAT 2000 System
with 6 ultrasonic detector heads. Additional
sounder model P100

Estimated Installation Date: Within 14 days of acceptance of this
quotation

Total Cost Including Installation: £595.00 excluding VAT

Payment Terms: 25% deposit on acceptance of quotation, balance
net within 30 days of completion of installation.

I trust this quotation will meet with your approval and have asked
out representative Nick Dawes to call upon you within the next
few days in case you should require any further information.

Yours sincerely,

John Millar
SCAT Security Ltd

Alan looked up from the letter. A blank form had appeared on his desk;
Nick's pen was poised.

'I'll want to read that,' said Alan.

Nick paused. 'Really? I've never had anyone read it before.'

Alan picked up the form and found himself looking at a document
printed in pale blue ink on bright yellow paper. Nick stretched out his
arms and legs and yawned.

AGREEMENT

Registered Office: Windsor House, Oglander Road, Mid Town, Midshire
Tel: 08991 871236   Vat Reg No 461 8466 992

SCAT Security Limited
Registered in England No 2260401739

Agreement No ....
Customer Name ....
Address ....
....
Postcode ....
Nature of Business ....
Sales Representative ....
Specification ....

Location of control
Location of siren(s)

Installation address ....

Estimated Date of Completion of Installation ....

Total cost
Including Installation £ .... excluding VAT
Deposit payable £ ....
(Receipt of which is hereby acknowledged)
Special Instructions ....

I accept the quotation herein for the supply and installation of a SCAT Electronic Security System as specified. I agree to be bound by the terms and conditions stated herein and overleaf.

Signature........................... Position...........
Name (in block capitals) ....
Date..
Signed on behalf of SCAT Security Limited ....
Date..

FOR OFFICE USE ONLY
Enquiry Source..... Credit Check......

Alan duly turned over the document to read the 'terms and conditions overleaf'.

AGREEMENT

Terms and Conditions for Supply and Installation

1.1   The customer shall provide without charge to the company adequate facilities for the storage of materials equipment and tools during the carrying out of the work and for a reasonable time before commencement and after completion.

1.2   Materials equipment and tools stored at the customer's premises shall be stored at the sole risk of the customer. In the event of destruction damage or theft of materials equipment and tools stored at the customers's premises the company shall be entitled to payment in full in respect thereof except that the customer shall not be liable for any loss occasioned solely by the negligence of the agents or employees of the company.

2.   The customer shall without charge make available electric power supply and other facilities necessary to carry out the work.

3.   The customer shall give the company access to the premises between the hours of 7.00 am and 5.00 pm Monday to Saturday for the purpose of doing anything which the company is under the terms of this agreement to do.

4.1   The company shall where reasonably possible conceal electrical cable beneath carpets and other floor covering but the quotation does not include the lifting and replacement of floorboards for the purpose of concealing cable.

4.2   Cables affixed to walls ceilings and doors shall be affixed to the surface thereof and the quotation does not include the cost of concealing such cable.

5.1   The acceptance of our quotation includes the acceptance of these terms and conditions.

5.2   This document sets out the whole of the agreement and undertaking between the parties.

6.1   Payment must be made within 30 days of completion of installation.

6.2   Overdue accounts shall be charged interest at the rate of 2.5% per month accruing daily.

---

7. No variation of these terms shall be binding upon the company unless agreed in writing and signed by a director of the company.

8. Installation dates are estimates only.

9.1 The equipment supplied is guaranteed for a period of 12 months from the date of installation against defects in workmanship and materials.

9.2 The company shall repair or replace the equipment at its discretion.

9.3 This guarantee is in lieu of any warranty implied by statute law as to fitness for purpose merchantability or compliance with any description.

10. No liability shall accrue to the company for damage or any other loss consequential on the malfunction of the system or circumnavigation of the system by an intruder.

11. The quotation herein is valid for a period of 30 days.

In many transactions one party is to receive from the other both goods and services. This is commonly known as a contract for work and materials. It is also referred to as a contract for the supply of goods and services – the terminology used in the modern Act which governs such contracts – and is therefore the terminology we shall use.

Everyday examples of contracts for the supply of goods and services include those for the installation of systems such as heating systems and burglar alarms, building contracts, and contracts for the installation of machinery. (In practice, building work except small-scale work is carried out on the basis of standard form industry contracts, the most widely used of which are the JCT contracts produced by a committee representing various bodies involved in the building industry such as architects and surveyors.)

We have seen in Chapter 10 how in a contract for the supply of services, the Supply of Goods and Services Act 1982 may imply terms into the contract relating to price, when the work is to be completed, and the standard of the work. Those implied terms apply also to a contract for goods and services. We have also seen, in Chapter 5, how terms are implied into a contract for the sale of goods relating to the merchantability of the goods, compliance with their description, and their fitness for a particular purpose. As regards the goods – using the word here in a very broad sense – received under a contract for goods and services, the Supply of Goods and Services Act implies almost identical terms into the contract. A supplier under a contract for goods and services therefore has two sets of obligations implied into the contract (except to the extent that he is able to exclude them, if at all): responsibility for the services provided and responsibility for the goods supplied.

Usually a contract for goods and services will require the supplier to do work to the property of the customer, although not always: a contract to paint a picture is a contract for goods and services. Working at the customer's premises introduces a number of important considerations.

SCAT Burglar Alarms is an example of a company which carries out work for both householders – the domestic market – and the commercial market. The company uses two standard agreements, one for each type of customer. This is because some of the clauses or phrasing suitable for a commercial contract are not entirely appropriate where customers are the general public, particularly as work for the commercial market often involves larger-scale projects. A further important reason for using different documentation for the commercial customer is that the company wishes to attempt to exclude the implied terms as to merchantability, description, and fitness for purpose; and, as with a contract for the sale of goods, in a consumer contract for the supply of goods and services these cannot be excluded.

The agreement presented by the alarm company's representative to Alan Taylor for his signature contained several important clauses.

Storage of materials, equipment and tools

1. *The customer shall provide without charge to the company adequate facilties for the storage of materials equipment and tools during the carrying out of the work and for a reasonable time before commencement and after completion.*

   Materials equipment and tools stored at the customer's premises shall be stored at the sole risk of the customer. In the event of destruction damage or theft of materials equipment and tools stored at the customer's premises the company shall be entitled to payment in full in respect thereof except that the customer shall not be liable for any loss occasioned solely by the negligence of the agents or employees of the company.

One of the authors worked for a period of time for a company supplying and installing cavity wall insulation in both private homes and commercial premises such as warehouses and offices. Often the average householder had no concept of what would be involved in the work to be carried out and, perhaps not unnaturally, had given no thought to the logistics. The customer might be somewhat put out to find workmen creating an obstruction on the driveway and humping bags of materials into her neat and tidy home. Having been seduced by visions of the wonderful benefits to be conferred by her new patio doors she may be surprisingly unreasonable about the disturbance caused by the carrying out of the work. Storage of materials overnight on the driveway can lead to the very reasonable complaint that it obstructs access to the garage, but moving the materials to the side can be met with the complaint that you are killing the grass!

Theft of materials from premises where work is being carried out is a major problem for contractors, especially in building works; hence the clause to make the customer liable for loss of materials. The company should, of course, have insurance to cover such losses but the item may be of comparatively small value, such as a handtool, and its loss would be too small to justify making an insurance claim. These are good reasons for inserting a clause into the contract which, if nothing else, encourages the customer to take some elementary security precautions at his premises and to keep an eye on the tools and materials.

Where the work undertaken is a large-scale project for a commercial customer, a clause in the supplier's standard form agreement may require the customer to insure the supplier's materials.

Use of electricity

2. *The customer shall without charge make available electric power supply and other facilities necessary to carry out the work.*

People are naturally wary of running up high electricity bills. Most customers are reasonable people. However, there are a tiny minority who will be very unhappy to find a stranger is using their electricity, and some of them who are not technically minded may have wild ideas about the amount of power used by electrical tools with which they are unfamiliar. The customer will be fussing round them and asking: 'Will you be using the electricity for much longer? I want to put the washing machine on.' This can be an unnecessary distraction and a source of pressure to complete the work in undue haste. In a bad case it may be helpful to point out the relevant clause in the agreement.

It is possible to pre-empt some of the problems that can crop up where work is to be carried out, by briefly going over the clauses when the deal is struck, and bringing to the customer's attention what will be involved – although from the sales point of view it may be preferable to do this after the customer has signed the agreement!

Agreed hours of work

3. *The customer shall give the company access to the premises between the hours of 7.00 am and 5.00 pm Monday to Saturday for the purpose of doing anything which the company is under the terms of this agreement entitled to do.*

This is something to wave under the nose of the customer who says it is not convenient for the engineers to come again tomorrow because he is going to visit his mother/show his blooms at the flower show/go to the January sales.

One assumes that the company does not envisage having to carry out the work outside their normal working hours, but suppose due to staff sickness the work falls behind and the company needs its staff to work extra hours to catch up?

In order to minimise disruption to the customer it may sometimes be necessary to work evenings or weekends, for example on shop premises where the work cannot be carried out when customers are coming and going. This would need to be specifically agreed between the parties and the arrangements spelt out in the agreement. The customer may also want the work to be carried out outside a company's normal working hours in order to complete it more quickly than would otherwise be the case. Again, this must be spelt out between the parties and recorded in the agreement. (The customer who wanted a job done as soon as possible may then be unhappy to find workmen banging about at 10 o'clock at night.)

Description of services

4. *The company shall where reasonably possible conceal electrical cable beneath carpets and other floor covering but the quotation does not include the lifting and replacement of floorboards for the purpose of concealing cable.*

    Cables affixed to walls ceilings and doors shall be affixed to the surface thereof and the quotation does not include the cost of concealing such cable.

In both a contract for services and a contract for goods and services it is most important to spell out what the customer is to receive under the contract. In the case of a sale of goods the customer can probably inspect a sample of the goods if not the actual goods themselves; but usually with a contract for the supply of services the customer has only a description. Naturally, the salesperson will have concentrated on bringing out for the customer the benefits, the desirability, of making their purchase. Some of the less attractive aspects of what they are to receive may only become apparent when the work is in hand.

Clause 4, concerning the fixing of electrical cables, is directed towards the kind of problem that can arise where the work involves installation. It may not have occurred to the customer that the installation of a burglar alarm system will necessitate the fixing of a considerable quantity of cable. As the work commences and the customer gets a better picture of what is involved, their response might be: 'We would have thought the price included you doing *XYZ*'. The customer can then be referred to the contract.

Making good

The customer who bothers to read the document may not pick up that there is no 'making good' clause. Where installation work is to be carried out it may be that some damage will necessarily be caused to the building or to decorations. For example, where a cable is to be inserted through a wall to a bell box installed on the exterior of the building, even the most skilled and careful craftsperson may inevitably cause some damage to the decor in performing such a task. Where this occurs the customer may be disappointed that there is no attempt by the workpeople to make good such damage, that it falls to the customer to do so. It is possible that a judge would say that the job must be carried out to a reasonable standard and that there is an implied term that the installer will make good the damage. But in order to price competitively the supplier may not include this in the work provided. In such a case it would be prudent to insert a clause to which the customer assents expressly declaring that the price does not include making good.

In many instances where work is carried out to premises it may be necessary to state who will be responsible for the clearing of the site after the work is completed, including removal of debris or discarded packaging materials.

Pricing

The contract for goods and services gives rise to more disputes between the parties over pricing than other types of agreement. This is due to the necessity to work out how long the work will take and also how much material will be used.

In a contract for goods and services we often find use of pricing according to 'estimates' and 'quotations'. Unfortunately, many consumers and some small businesses bandy the terms about without knowing their meaning. A not uncommon type of grievance about which clients consult their solicitor concerns the tradesperson who has given them a 'quotation' for work and then on completion of the work has presented a bill higher than the quotation. Sadly, during the course of the interview, the client may refer to both an estimate and a quotation, using the terms as if they are interchangeable. The solicitor has to explain to the client that a quotation, unless the agreement provides otherwise, involves a firm price, whereas an estimate is just that: an estimate of what the price will be rather than a final figure.

However, where the price takes the form of an estimate the supplier is not at liberty to then charge a figure which bears no relationship to that given. Nor is he expected by the law to have assessed the cost with precise accuracy; the customer will be legally liable to pay a sum reasonably close to the price he was given. What is reasonably close depends on all the circumstances and is something about which the parties will probably argue.

Checklist

The following points should be considered when drawing up a contract for work and materials. Remember that each of them is almost certain to have several aspects:

- The parties
- Exclusion or limitation of liability
- Price
- Payment
- *Force majeure*
- Storage of materials
- Variation
- Supply by customer of electricity and other services
- Specification/description
- Passing of ownership in the materials
- Risk in the materials
- Access to premises
- Sample
- Guarantee
- Duration/completion date
- Rules or implied terms to oust
- Arbitration
- Other matters.

Glossary

Acceptance. A clear assent to the terms of an offer

Actionable. Giving cause to pursue a legal remedy

Agent. A person who acts on behalf of another (the Principal) with power to bind that other

Breach of contract. Failure or refusal by a party to a contract to observe his obligations under the contract

Caveat emptor. Latin for 'Buyer beware'

Condition. A major term of the contract, breach of which entitles the other party to regard the contract as being at an end

Consideration. That which a party to a contract receives from the other party in return for his promise or act

Contract in restraint of trade. A contract by which a person undertakes to restrict in the future with whom he will do business or the manner in which he will do business

Contract for services. A contract under which one of the parties is to perform work for another but in doing so is not an employee of that other

Contract of service. The more traditional term for a contract of employment.

Counter offer. The response of an offeree to an offer, stating terms which differ from the terms of the offer made to him

Damages. A sum of money payable as compensation

Exclusion clause. A clause excluding or modifying legal obligation

Force majeure clause. A clause making provision for unforeseen events or for matters beyond the control of the party concerned

Hire purchase contract. A contract under which goods are hired out to a person who has an option to purchase them for nominal consideration after a specified number of instalments have been paid

Intermediate stipulation. A contractual obligation, the remedies for breach of which depend upon the consequences of the breach

Liquidated damages. A sum specified in the contract as the amount payable as compensation in the event of a breach of contract

Merchantable quality.   Fit for the purpose for which goods of that type are commonly bought

Nominal consideration.   Token payment

Offer.   A statement of terms by which the party making it appears willing to be bound

Offeree.   The party to whom an offer is made

Offeror.   The party who makes an offer

Order for specific performance.   An order of a court requiring the person concerned to carry out a contract

Penalty clause.   A clause under which a sum is specified as the amount payable in compensation for breach of contract but which is not a genuine pre-estimate of the loss

Principal.   The person on whose behalf an agent acts

Quantum meruit.   Latin for the basis on which a person may claim a reasonable price for what the other party has received

Representation.   A statement of fact intended to induce a person to enter into a contract

Rescission.   The setting aside of a contract, so that as far as possible the parties are put back into their pre-contract position

Reservation of title clause.   A clause under which the seller of goods retains ownership until some condition is fulfilled, eg the goods are paid for

Standard form contract.   A contract using standard terms offered by one of the parties to different contracting parties and not individually negotiated

Tort.   A wrong committed against another which gives that other person a remedy in civil (as opposed to criminal) law

Vicarious liability.   The liability of one person for the wrongs of another

Warranty.   A subsidiary term of the contract, breach of which entitles the innocent party to recover damages for harm caused by the breach, but which does not entitle the innocent party to treat the contract as being at an end

Further Reading from Kogan Page

Be Your Own Company Secretary, A J Scrine, 2nd edition, 1990

The Business Guide to Effective Writing, J Fletcher and D F Gowing, 1989

How to Write a Staff Manual: A Guide for Managers, S L Brock and S R Cabell, 1990

Law for the Small Business: The Daily Telegraph Guide, 7th edition, Patricia Clayton, 1991

Readymade Business Letters, Jim Denning, 1988

Kogan Page publishes many titles on running and managing a business or department. A complete list is available from 120 Pentonville Road, London N1 9JN; 071-278 0433.

Index